RENEW!

Become a Better
— and More Authentic —
Writing Teacher

SHAWNA COPPOLA

FOREWORD BY THOMAS NEWKIRK

STENHOUSE PUBLISHERS
PORTLAND, MAINE

Stenhouse Publishers
www.stenhouse.com

Credits
Figure 2.3: From *The Craft of Revision*, 2nd ed., by Donald M. Murray. Copyright © 1995. Used with permission of Harcourt Brace Publishing.
Figure 2.4: From *A Writer Teaches Writing*, 2nd ed., by Donald M. Murray. Copyright © 2003. Used with permission of Cengage Learning.
Figures 2.9 and 2.10: Images © 2014 by Marla Frazee

Library of Congress Cataloging-in-Publication Data is available for this title

Cover and interior design by Blue Design (www.bluedes.com)

Manufactured in the United States of America

PRINTED ON 30% PCW
RECYCLED PAPER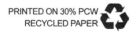

23 22 21 20 19 18 17   9 8 7 6 5 4 3 2 1

For Margaret Shirley

CONTENTS

Foreword

Here is how you should read this book.

With a cup of tea, on an unhurried weekend afternoon, away from the din of football—the kind of time you'd like to spend with an outgoing friend with an irrepressible sense of humor. That is what you will get with Shawna Coppola's *Renew! Become a Better—and More Authentic—Writing Teacher.* Relax and enjoy an afternoon's reflection on how to break out of rigid prescriptions and orthodoxies that limit writing instruction, with some illuminating side trips into parenting.

This book helps cut through the clutter of rules and materials that obscure good writing instruction. Now, forty-three years after the publication of Donald Graves' *Writing: Teachers and Children at Work,* there is so much "stuff" available—scoring guides, rubrics, lists of mini-lessons, writing prompts, charts outlining the steps of the writing process, checklists—you name it. A Google search for writing rubrics comes up with 1.2 million sites. So much to entrap you. The ink was barely dry on Graves' book when educators began debating (to his wry amusement) whether it was better to do the "Three Step Graves" or the "Five Step Graves." Early on he recognized that "the enemy is orthodoxy."

It's easy to forget how improvisational the "writing process" was when Graves started his landmark study of children's writing in Atkinson, New Hampshire. For example, his work opened the door for the use of "invented spelling" in the early grades—but when the study began, he and his team *had never even heard of the concept.* It took a trip to a Belmont, Massachusetts, classroom and some reading of Carol Chomsky to get an idea of how it might work. One of the lead teachers in the study, Maryellen Giacobbe, showed some of this writing to her first graders, leading one of them to pronounce: "This is cinchy." And they were off.

There was a lightness, an experimentalism, a responsiveness in this very early instruction. Don, Lucy Calkins, and Susan Sowers would sit down with the teachers at the end of the day to discuss how things were going and brainstorm possible changes. One thing that sustained them was the very unpredictability of teaching and learning.

This book embodies that sense of improvisation and ultimately not being limited by "stuff." It's being willing to trust our responses to student writing—what engages, delights, or confuses us—and not capitulating to rigid rubrics with their false sense of objectivity. (If we need additional data on the folly of rating scales, my book *The Art of Slow Reading* has a higher Amazon rating than *King Lear*.) It's being open to a larger role for art and drawing in the writing process. It is refusing to be stuck and complacent, refusing to settle, refusing to teach by someone else's rules that may not fit our students.

It all reminds me of a conversation a literacy consultant had with a teacher who was reluctant to try a new approach to reading. "Try it," the consultant urged. "It doesn't have to be perfect." And the teacher answered, "But you don't get it. For me, it does have to be perfect." To which the consultant responded, "How do you know what you do now is perfect?"

Perfection is not a human quality. But we can understand that teacher's reluctance to move out of familiar routines and take on something new. As William James noted over a century ago, in the matter of change we are all, by our nature, conservatives. But "renewal" can be exhilarating. Renewal—to develop what John Keats famously called a "negative capability," when we are "capable of being in uncertainties,

mysteries, doubts, without any irritable reaching after fact and reason."
Renewal—to be new again, to rediscover that lightness of being, that
willingness to set out and trust that we can find our way, even if it is
not well marked.

But like all travel, it helps to have a companion, and I think you will
find Shawna a good one. She is open about her own teaching and parenting journey, her own occasional resistance to change, her reluctance
to be the writing model she knew she should be. She has good practical
advice, drawn from her own teaching. It's a personal and candid book.

Brew a cup of tea and join her.

Tom Newkirk

Acknowledgments

It's quite easy to think about writing acknowledgments while waiting to pick up your kid from swim practice or while avoiding doing the *actual* work of writing a book—but it's quite difficult to sit down to write them. For one thing, you don't want to leave anyone out whose contributions have led to your book coming to fruition; for another, you have a few hours to kill before school lets out, so you can't help but fantasize about taking a nap instead. (Just being real here.)

I can't acknowledge the many people who have helped guide me toward this moment without first thanking Gert Nesin and her sister, Janet Nesin-Reynolds, whose thinking, teaching, and enormous respect for children made me the educator I am today. Not a day goes by that I don't think about the lessons they taught me so many years ago.

To the many mentors I've had over the years as a student at the University of New Hampshire—in particular, Tom Newkirk, Paula Salvio, Ruth Wharton-McDonald, and Grant Cioffi—thank you for always pushing me to think in ways I never before considered. (We miss you, Grant.)

To Kathy Collins: thank you for "writing" alongside me during our regular jaunts to our favorite local coffee shops. (I put *writing* in quotes because we both know we spent more time gossiping, checking our social media feeds, and psychoanalyzing Kanye West during these "writing" sessions.) If I could include an awesome gif here that perfectly encapsulates our friendship, you know I would!

To Amy Rasmussen, Dylan Teut, Christopher Lehman, and my Educator Collaborative Mini-Think Tank colleagues: thank you for reading portions of my early drafts and offering me your support, encouragement, and valuable suggestions for how to make this project better. I owe you one.

To my mom, dad, and brothers, Jamieson and Nicholas: if you don't purchase and ruthlessly plug my book, you can forget about Secret Santa this year. (P.S. Love you!)

To the students, faculty, and staff at Rollinsford Grade School, especially my principal, Katherine Lucas: I learn from you each and every day. Thank you for your curiosity, your kindness, and your humor.

To my wonderful husband, David, my elegant "sun," Gianna, and my feisty "firecracker," Sydney: ALL THE FEELS. I am the luckiest person in the world to count you as my family. You never fail to make me a better human. Also, please stop asking me what's for dinner.

To my colleagues at Stenhouse, especially Jay Kilburn, Chris Downey, Grace Makley, Louisa Irele, and Dan Tobin: thank you for believing in me and for welcoming me so warmly into the Stenhouse family. I'm grateful to be a part of it.

I must save my last words of thanks for my editor, Maureen Barbieri. Maureen was unaware of this until now, but she came into my life at *precisely* the right moment. Although she is a gifted editor who always succeeds in lifting me as a writer, she is, more importantly, a trusted and valued friend whose presence greatly tempered the grief from which I was reeling after an enormous personal loss. For that, Maureen, I will be forever indebted to you. Thank you.

Introduction

My husband, David, and I sat on our therapist's couch, trying—unsuccessfully, mind you—to appear much more comfortable than we were both feeling. Not only was it next to impossible to keep our bodies upright due to the sinkhole that threatened to draw us together at any moment; the fact was, sitting in a therapist's office as a result of the difficulty our family—in particular, our youngest daughter—was experiencing was nowhere we'd ever imagined we'd be. After months of tears, frustration, and worry, the time had come for us to face our family challenges head-on—to avoid falling into the sinkhole of modern-day parenting.

Our therapist leaned forward in her chair and regarded us kindly, her hands clasped gently in her lap. "Please don't think you are *bad parents*," she said softly. "You are *good parents* to the 80 percent of children out there. Sydney just happens to be part of that 20 percent that you must . . . adjust for."

David and I glanced at each other, partially relieved by her assurance (*Yes! We don't* completely *stink!*) and partially daunted by the prospect of parenting Sydney in a completely different way than we had parented our oldest daughter, Gianna. (To get a sense of their differences in personality, I once wrote a poem [Figure 1] about my two daughters called "The Sun and the Firecracker." Guess which one is which.)

Over the course of the next several months, my husband and I would learn that instead of trying to reason with Sydney when she was acting combative, we would need to acknowledge, without judgment, what

Sydney was feeling and simply *listen* to her. Instead of getting angry with her for resisting our request that she do her chores *that minute*, we would need to learn to collaborate on a plan for finishing chores that allowed Sydney some voice and choice—and to reflect on why we felt the need to impose our own time limits on her. As simple as these examples may sound, we weren't learning to make mere *tweaks* to our parenting behaviors—what we were learning was that, in many cases, what we thought we knew about what it meant to be a "good" parent was being turned entirely on its head.

You may be rolling your eyes at what we learned throughout our family therapy sessions (e.g., "When I was a kid, my parents simply told me what's what, and I LISTENED, damn it!"), but for my husband and me, the strategies we learned and practiced allowed for a much more peaceful, relaxed, and joyful family dynamic. As difficult as it was for us, initially, to face the fact that we didn't know everything there was to know about being effective parents, this "rethinking" of our parenting empowered David and me to think critically about our attitudes and behaviors—as well as those of our daughters—resulting in a revision of our parenting behaviors and, ultimately, a greater understanding of each family member's needs, desires, and quirks.

My husband and I gained some other unexpected benefits through rethinking and revising our parenting behaviors. Not only did the strategies we learned benefit our interactions with Sydney, our little "firecracker," they *equally affected* our interactions with Gianna in an enormously positive way. As our therapist had delicately explained to us so many months prior, the way we were parenting wasn't necessarily "wrong" or "bad"; for most children, the ways in which we dealt with typical parent-child situations was satisfactory, and would have likely resulted in the desired outcomes (e.g., brushing teeth before bed, getting to bed by a certain time). The more delicate, difficult truth was that the way we were parenting wasn't effective for every child—Sydney included. Not only that, but the strategies we had employed as parents

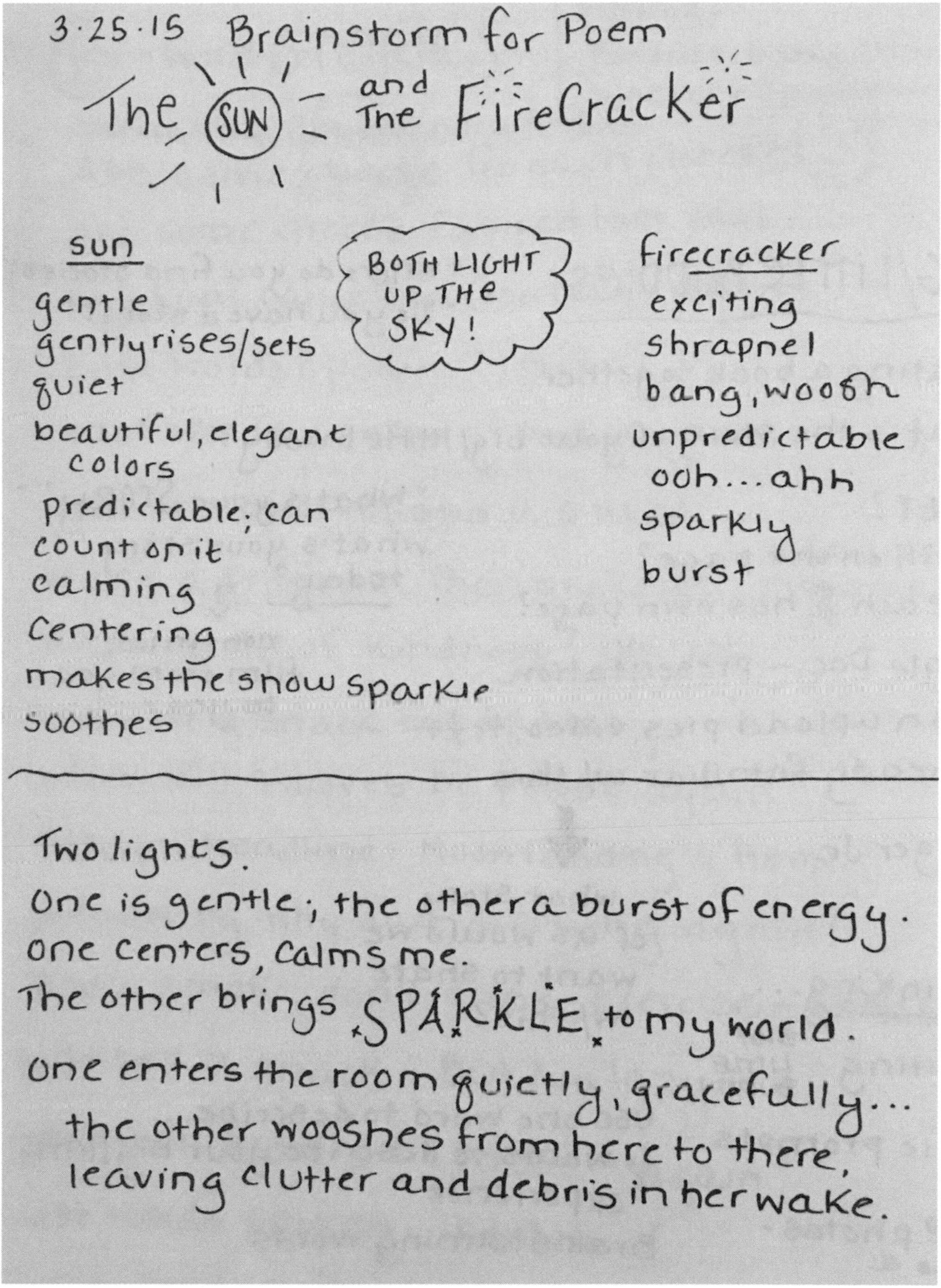

3·25·15 Brainstorm for Poem

The (SUN) and The FireCracker

sun
gentle
gently rises/sets
quiet
beautiful, elegant
  colors
predictable; can
count on it
calming
centering
makes the snow sparkle
soothes

BOTH LIGHT
UP THE
SKY!

firecracker
exciting
shrapnel
bang, woosh
unpredictable
ooh...ahh
sparkly
burst

Two lights.
One is gentle; the other a burst of energy.
One centers, calms me.
The other brings SPARKLE to my world.
One enters the room quietly, gracefully...
  the other wooshes from here to there,
leaving clutter and debris in her wake.

FIGURE 1
Early draft of "The Sun and the Firecracker"

3

were simply what we'd learned through osmosis (and were perhaps influenced by books we had read years earlier, when we had time to read such things). In learning more effective ways to communicate with Sydney through our therapy sessions, David and I had built a repertoire for communicating with Gianna as well—not to mention for communicating with each other.

What does this have to do with teaching, you ask? In short: everything. For so many of us, the strategies we typically use to instruct our students are "good" practices—for a sizeable chunk of our population. I use the term *good* loosely, to mean that such instructional practices won't necessarily *harm* most students (just as the practices that my husband and I used to parent our oldest daughter, Gianna, weren't necessarily harmful to her). But in order for us to be truly effective—for *as many of our students as possible*—I would argue, much as our family therapist did with us, that it is crucial to routinely examine our practices in light of the children we have in front of us and adjust them as needed.

David and I were lucky; it was fairly easy for us to recognize that our default parenting style was simply not working for Sydney. As classroom teachers, we are not always so lucky. Oftentimes, when things aren't working, we are quick to place blame on students: they're "unmotivated," "lazy," or "reluctant." Rarely are we willing to turn the lens on ourselves to rethink—and if necessary, revise—the practices that have become, over time, our "default" practices.

This book is our means for doing just that. Consider it a professional therapy "toolbox." In it, I will share the framework I have developed over fifteen-plus years of experience as an educator to help us examine, or "rethink," some of our most pervasive educational practices. This framework will also help us ask the questions necessary in order to revise our practice so that it is effective for *all* students rather than most.

Chapter 1 will make the case in greater detail for why it is important for us to engage in this challenging, yet incredibly invigorating, work.

Chapters 2–5 will examine some of the most ubiquitous practices that we, as teachers of writers, employ within our classrooms, including how we typically assess writing as well as how many of us teach the writing process. Finally, Chapter 6 will take a critical look at our role as teachers of writers and what we can do to nurture a writerly life of our own, thus renewing our instructional practice.

What if David and I had never sought a therapist's help, consequently leading us to rethink and revise our parenting practice? We would have continued to parent as we always had, we would've hit more than a few roadblocks along the way, Sydney's combative behavior would've likely increased over time, and Gianna would've (likely) received less and less of our parental attention. Ultimately, however, we all would've probably emerged from the whole experience just fine.

We wanted much more for our family than "fine." And as educators, we want much more than "fine" for our students . . . don't we?

In the interest of being transparent, I'll say this: rethinking and revising our practice will not be easy. In some instances, it will be a downright cringeworthy process. At times you will find yourself vigorously nodding your head; at other times, you'll want to slam this book shut and chuck it across the room. But that's okay. I'll still invite you in and offer you a safe, quiet place in which to rethink, revise, and ultimately renew your professional practice.

So come, have a seat. Get as comfortable as you can. And above all, avoid the sinkhole.

*Our world has been so tremendously enlarged and
complicated, our horizons so widened and our sympathies
so stimulated, by the changes in our surroundings and
habits . . . that a school curriculum which does not show
this same growth can only be very partially successful.*

—John Dewey and Evelyn Dewey

Why It's Important to Continually Rethink, Revise, & Renew Our Practice as Teachers of Writers

We educators just *love* John Dewey, don't we? (See Figure 1.1.) If he were alive and on Twitter, he would probably have over thirty thousand followers. We'd all be clamoring to participate in his monthly Twitter chat, *#deweysez*. His blog would get thousands of hits per day. John Dewey is so beloved within the world of education—and has been for well over a century—that to quote him in front of other educators is to have your stock instantly go up; your credibility *skyrockets*. In popular

FIGURE 1.1
Dewey and his instant credibility
superpowers (not pictured)

culture terms, he's like the Tom Hanks of the education world.

For those of you unfamiliar with Dewey, he was a renowned American philosopher and psychologist who wrote often throughout the late nineteenth century and early twentieth century about education, democracy, and social reform. In fact, he is often credited with some of the most quotable statements about education with which we teachers are familiar, although most of them have been breezily modified to suit our simpler, more Instagram-worthy tastes. (A brief sampling can be found in Table 1.1.)

TABLE 1.1
John Dewey "Quotes" That Never Were—and Their Actual Counterparts

Instagram-Worthy Dewey "Quote"	What Dewey Actually Said/Wrote
"Education is not preparation for life; education is life itself."	"Cease conceiving of education as mere preparation for later life, and make it the full meaning of the present life." ("Self-Realization as the Moral Ideal," 1893)
"We do not learn from experience … we learn from reflecting on experience."	"[Education] … means that the various parts of the information acquired are grasped in their relation to one another—a result that is attained only when acquisition is accompanied by constant reflection upon the meaning of what is studied." (*How We Think*, 1910)
"If we teach today's students as we taught yesterday's we rob them of tomorrow."	"Our world has been so tremendously enlarged and complicated, our horizons so widened and our sympathies so stimulated, by the changes in our surroundings and habits … that a school curriculum which does not show this same growth can only be very partially successful." (*Schools of To-morrow*, 1915)

One of my favorite Dewey quotes, which—as it turns out—was most likely never actually *uttered* by the man, is this one, because it pretty much sums up my entire book in one simple sentence:

> *If we teach today's students as we taught yesterday's, we rob them of tomorrow.*

In Instagram-worthy collage form, it might look something like the image in Figure 1.2.

Now, I *could* conceivably tweet this quote or post it on my blog, thereby saving my editor hundreds of hours of effort, but that would be too darn easy. (Plus, hardly anyone follows my blog.) And the quote, while certainly snappy and chock-full of wisdom, really doesn't paint the *comprehensive* picture that I would like to paint in order to inspire my fellow colleagues to move to action.

You see, I believe with every fiber of my being that it is essential for educators to do everything we can to avoid becoming complacent in our work. The minute—no, the very *second*—that we believe we have done all we can for our student writers—that we have learned all there is to learn about, say, teaching them how to write satisfying conclusions, or how to generate ideas for writing—well, that is also the very second we become less effective.

Before you slam this book shut and toss it through the nearest

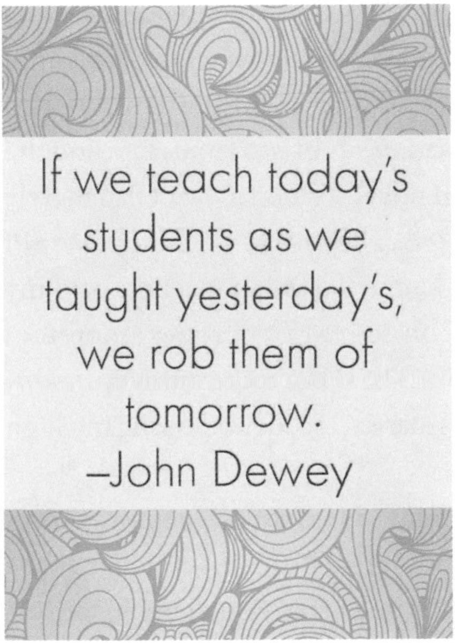

FIGURE 1.2
One of my favorite John Dewey "quotes"

window, hear me out. Despite what you may be thinking, I'm not a glutton for punishment. I do think there are moments—dozens, if not hundreds, of them each year—when we can (and should) celebrate our teaching successes. After all, teaching is heartbreakingly, back-achingly, mind-numbingly difficult work. Teaching students to write well—and to *love* it? Close to impossible. But if we are truly willing to honor the individuality of our student writers, the uniqueness of each community of learners, and the ever-changing nature of our global landscape, we must continually rethink, revise, and renew our practice. Otherwise—to paraphrase Dewey—we rob "today's" students of the *tomorrow today's students deserve.*

What Do I Mean by This?

Let me paint a picture for you by telling you about my favorite high school English teacher, Mr. Carson (a pseudonym). Oh, how my classmates and I worshiped Mr. C in his pastel-colored slacks and matching sweater vests! Among the most academically minded of us were those whose primary mission it was to elicit one of his signature wry smiles due to a clever remark about a novel's theme or an astute observation about one of its characters. Although these smiles were most often bestowed on the males in our class, I was one of the few females who regularly elicited them with my uncanny ability to appear as though I had carefully read all of our assigned novels (when in fact I had merely skimmed the CliffsNotes versions). As a result, Mr. C became one of my favorite teachers. This usually happened when teachers paid my awkward, adolescent self what I considered the proper amount of attention, but it was doubly true for Mr. C because of the status his attention gained me as one of the "smarter" students among my high school peers.

My adoration continued throughout my junior and senior years of high school and followed me as an English Teaching student at the University of New Hampshire. Each time I envisioned my future career, I pictured myself in my own classroom, surrounded by my own adoring students, discussing the ruinous nature of unchanging love in *Wuthering Heights*—essentially, as the female version of Mr. Carson, but with better style and less of a mustache. I could barely wait until my senior year, when I could spend an entire semester soaking up the wisdom and skill of Mr. C as I observed his process from a closer vantage point.

I'll never forget the day when I began my observation period of Mr. Carson, who was teaching one of his AP English classes at my old high school. It had been just a few short years since I had been in this very same classroom discussing *The Scarlet Letter*. As I sat in a seat adjacent to the man my former classmates and I had so revered, I remember thinking how suspiciously similar their discussion was to the one *we* had had about the vengeful Roger Chillingworth, Hester Prynne's cuckolded husband.

Now, you may be thinking that I was foolish to feel suspicious. After all, Roger Chillingworth is an important character in *The Scarlet Letter*, an evil contrast to the impulsive but tenderhearted Hester. Isn't it likely that English classrooms all over the country would have these same kinds of discussions about him?

Well, yes, maybe—but there's more.

I glanced over at the notes Mr. Carson had laid out on the desk in front of him and was surprised to see that the yellow-lined paper he had used to write out his discussion questions was tattered and discolored around the edges, much like an old treasure map found in the bottom of someone's attic trunk (see Figure 1.3).

When I peered closer at Mr. C's trademark scrawl, I saw that, at the top, the paper was dated *ten years prior* and contained very few discernible revisions.

I felt like I'd suddenly lost my appetite. I sat back in my chair and disengaged from the discussion, attempting to reconcile in my head this man, who had been using almost the *exact same* notes to generate

FIGURE 1.3
Not the actual paper, but . . . you get the idea.

a discussion about *The Scarlet Letter* for nearly half my life, with the teacher I had thought I wanted to be.

As hard as I tried to, I couldn't.

I think part of my reaction had to do with a feeling of betrayal. Our class discussions had always felt so organic, so *responsive* to our reactions to the reading. But not only did that morning's discussion echo the one my classmates and I had had four years earlier—in some cases, it seemed to match it *exactly*, right down to the joke Mr. Carson made about Chillingworth's "manhood." (I kid you not.)

Big deal, right? I mean, we all know—or know of—a Mr. Carson. At this point you might be thinking to yourself, *What's so wrong about sticking to a tried-and-true plan for a class discussion? Was Mr. Carson really such a bad teacher?*

That's the thing—just as there was nothing inherently "wrong" or "bad" about my husband and I as parents (see Introduction), there's nothing necessarily *wrong* or *bad* about Mr. Carson's teaching, or about any of the instructional practices I mention throughout the following chapters. But there are "good" teaching practices, and there are better, more powerful ones—ones that are far more authentic, engaging, and responsive to students.

Don't you want to be *better*? More powerful in your teaching?

I did. And I do.

The Power of Rethinking and Revising

Let's compare my experience with the beloved Mr. Carson with another one. Not too long ago, I was soaking in some of the amazing teaching and learning in one of the multiage fifth- and sixth-grade classes at Rollinsford Grade School in Rollinsford, New Hampshire, where I work as a K–6 literacy specialist. The students were discussing the mental strategies they had used to solve a multiplication problem and assessing which were most efficient. After the discussion, their teacher, Ms. Doherty, asked students to solve the problem using a newly taught strategy: the area model. I asked some of Ms. Doherty's students if I could watch them try to solve the problem using the strategy, as I had never heard of it and was eager to learn from them.

One student, Ruby, was using a small whiteboard to sketch out her model. I asked if I could take a photo of her work to help me later as I continued to process this particular problem-solving method. "Sure," she said, holding up her whiteboard so I could snap a good one with my phone (see Figure 1.4).

A few minutes later, as I was getting ready to leave the classroom, Ruby approached me, holding her whiteboard in her hands. "I just wanted to show you some of my revised thinking before you leave," she said (see Figure 1.5).

I shot an astonished look at my principal, Kate Lucas, who had also been visiting the class during that block. Kate's eyes widened and she put her hand to her mouth in disbelief. *Are you freaking kidding me?*

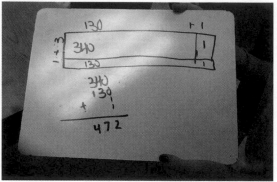

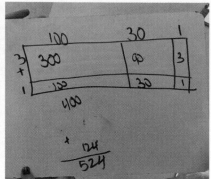

FIGURE 1.4
Ruby's whiteboard sketch

FIGURE 1.5
Ruby's revised thinking

our eyes asked each other. "Of course! I'd love to see it," I said, and listened to her explain how she had redrawn her model to solve the problem more efficiently. (Looking back, I can't for the life of me figure out the mathematical thinking behind Ruby's revision, but that's beside the point.)

Later, as Kate and I debriefed with each other about what we'd seen and heard in the classroom that morning, our smiles widened as our conversation turned to Ruby. With no prompting whatsoever, Ruby had taken it upon herself not only to *rethink* and *revise* her approach to the multiplication problem, but to show me, an infrequent visitor during math class, *how* she had done so. Ruby had clearly moved past the kind of thinking that is prevalent in so many classrooms—particularly in math classrooms—since the dawn of schooling: that there are *right* ways of thinking and there are *wrong* ways of thinking; that there are *right* answers and there are *wrong* answers; that school is about learning *facts* rather than learning to *think*.

Pretty powerful, right?

I can tell you with the utmost certainty that Ruby's inherent fabulousness alone is not behind her learning style, although that is quite possibly a mitigating factor. Ruby and her classmates have a model on which to draw. They are part of both a classroom and a wider learning community that is teeming with educators who consistently rethink and revise their practice and their assumptions about teaching and learning—who not only value critical thinking, problem solving, and healthy risk-taking, but who actively teach their students these skills. As surprised as I was to have Ruby approach me to show me her revised thinking, it is not uncommon for me to hear this kind of language at my school. Rethinking and revising the work we do across all areas has become a natural way for us, students *and* teachers, to learn, to reflect on that learning, and to make the necessary changes needed to help us renew our professional lives in a variety of ways. You won't find any tattered, discolored lesson plans here; they've long since been stored away—or in many cases, tossed directly into the trash.

So What?

How can this idea of renewal be such a powerful paradigm for teaching and learning? As I mentioned earlier, we live in an ever-changing global landscape. The pioneering thinker R. Buckminster Fuller developed what is known as the "Knowledge Doubling Curve," a concept that illustrates how exponentially the world's knowledge is growing over time (see Figure 1.6).

According to Fuller's paradigm, the amount of time it takes for us to increase our collective knowledge base by 100 percent will *continue to shrink the older we get.* David Russell Schilling, a researcher, consultant, and writer for the news website Industry Tap, estimates that our collective knowledge doubles, on average, approximately *every twelve months.* If this is true—or even *close* to being true—how can we, as educators, ever feel satisfied with teaching our students the same concepts, using the same methodologies and practices, that we have in the past?

As teachers of writers, we try to entice, convince, and cajole our students into revising their writing in order to improve it. I use the terms *entice, convince,* and *cajole* deliberately, because it is rare that teaching students to revise their work—let alone their thinking—is

FIGURE 1.6
Whoa.

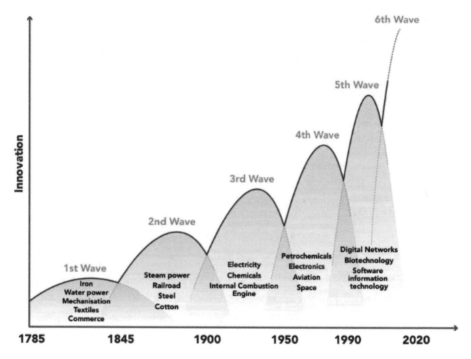

The Knowledge Doubling Curve

Source, The Natural Edge Project

easy. Of course, most students actually spontaneously revise as they compose, but for *extensive revision* of their work to become a habitual practice, effort, time, and not a small amount of coaxing are required.

The same could be said about our own professional lives. Most of us make little tweaks to our writing curriculum from year to year, from day to day, and, sometimes, from minute to minute. But how often do we *extensively* revise our practice? How often do we revise our assumptions about writing—and about our student writers?

A Suggested Framework

One way to ensure that we consistently rethink and revise our instructional practice as teachers of student writers is to use a framework that, with practice, will make it more likely for us to internalize the necessary mindset (see Table 1.2). Not only will such a framework sustain our students as they move through the shifting world in which they live as writers, it will also empower *us* as learners through the regular renewal of our teaching practice.

TABLE 1.2
A Framework for Rethinking, Revising, & Renewing Our Practice

RETHINK	REVISE	RENEW
Questions to ask: What "story" does [practice] tell about writing? What merit does it have? How does it fit into what we know about children? About learning? Does this match my current students' needs and interests? Is [practice] what I would want for myself as a learner? What do other voices in the field have to say about [practice] or about alternative practices?	Questions to ask: How can we modify or revise our practice in order to tell a more authentic, more engaging, or more powerful story about writing? What do today's students need and want? How do I know? How might I incorporate students' needs and wants into my practice?	Revitalize our practice by continually engaging in this framework of thinking—and in doing so, passing that energy onto our students!

As I warned in my introduction, this sort of work is not easy. There's a reason we are still quoting Dewey (or Dewey-*ish* statements) a hundred years after they first materialized. They continue to inspire and motivate us despite the countercurrent of educational reform. But if we, as educators, are serious about moving our practice from "good" to "better," if we are committed to avoiding complacency, we must do more than invoke platitudes: we must also be willing to take some serious action.

The renewal—*our* renewal—begins now.

If you forget how I have screwed up, I will
forget how you have screwed up.

—Donald Murray

. . . .

CHAPTER 2

Renew How We Teach Writing Process

This is the story of how I screwed up the teaching of writing process.

During my first five years in the classroom, I would spend hours each summer crafting posters highlighting "the" writing process that I would post in the most coveted spot in my entire classroom: the wall above my chalkboard. (This should give you a sense of how old I am.) I would use my poster-making skills—honed during the year and a half I spent as a resident assistant at the University of New Hampshire—to beautifully handwrite the words *prewrite, draft, revise, edit,* and *publish* onto cardstock using a black, chisel-tipped permanent marker. I would then carefully tape the cardstock to the wall in orderly, perfectly spaced intervals (see Figure 2.1).

FIGURE 2.1
Artist's rendering of the handwritten posters from my classroom, circa 2001

This is how I was taught to teach writing: as a series of predetermined steps that are taken by "real" writers. At least, this is how I *thought* I was taught to teach writing. As a University of New Hampshire alumna, I was sure that this was what Don Graves—pioneer of the workshop approach to teaching writing—would have wanted. I can't tell you exactly how I acquired this misguided notion. I'm sure the poor soul who taught the one course on teaching writing I took before becoming a teacher would be horrified by the way I neatly packaged Graves' pedagogical wisdom before imposing it upon my hapless students.

Needless to say, I was so married to this particular process that I can actually recall telling students that they *could not draft* before they had finished their prewriting—because that, after all, was how "the" writing process worked. If that weren't bad enough, the way I taught students to "prewrite" was hopelessly inauthentic, in that their prewriting almost always took the form of a web (bleh), a story map (ugh) or—perhaps most cringeworthy of all—a hamburger essay graphic organizer. (More on these, along with other tools we frequently use to teach students to write, in Chapter 4.)

How I taught students to draft—the next step in the writing process, according to my handy-dandy posters—wasn't much better. I had little patience for the time it takes to draft something of substance, and as soon as I had successfully conferred with each student about what he or she was writing, I considered the drafting part of the process, for the most part, complete.

Then, of course, came the revising stage. "Today we are going to revise our drafts," I would announce to the class, as if I were the author of their personal narratives, their fiction stories, or their feature articles and, as such, had divine control over their processes. I would then proceed to teach a mini-lesson on "revising" that would ironically take up so much class time that students had only a handful of minutes to *actually* work on revising their drafts.

And so on and so forth; you get the drift. Clearly, I didn't have a single clue about how to teach student writers.

It didn't matter that I hated asking students to postpone drafting until they had done a sufficient amount of "prewriting" (i.e., filling out a graphic organizer). It didn't matter that, when I wrote, I revised as I drafted—*just as I am doing now*—and not always once I had completed an entire draft. It didn't matter that, even though my students "published" 90 percent of their drafted pieces (by my divine decree), 90 percent of what I wrote on my own time went unpublished. It didn't matter, because this step-by-step process—prewriting, drafting, revising, editing, and publishing—was *what Don Graves would have wanted*.

The joke, of course, is that my writing workshop was far from what Don Graves (or my other workshop mentors, among them Donald Murray and Katie Wood Ray) would ever want to see in a classroom.

Although all three educators—as well as hundreds of other literacy experts—have referred to "the writing process" in their respective works, each has done so in a holistic way, alongside the unspoken caveat that "the" writing process does not actually exist; that there is, in fact, no "one" way that writers compose. And yet how many posters like the ones I so carefully crafted each summer are pinned to Pinterest boards or sold at teacher supply stores? How many classrooms have the same five steps of "the" writing process posted over their Smartboards or in other conspicuous classroom spaces, organized in the same tired order? Some of these resources have even added a *sixth* step to the process— wholly separate from revising and editing—called "rewriting," during which students are directed to literally *rewrite their entire composition* (using a black pen, in some cases), as if students didn't resent writing enough (see Figure 2.2).

Rethinking "The" Writing Process

The story I was, in effect, telling my students about writing—and the story that continues to be told in the majority of classrooms all over the country, despite what we'd like to believe—is that all writers follow the same fixed process, that certain steps in the process cannot happen without completing other steps first. (If you doubt my assertion, check out the following videos about "the" writing process on YouTube, which, combined, have amassed over 148,000 views as of this writing: https://youtu.be/71Y2uIyJM4g, https://youtu.be/JPUh9mfSqWU, and https://youtu.be/iobYihZ4FvQ). But while this linear movement through the stages of writing may mirror the experience of some writers, it certainly doesn't do so for all or even most of them.

Subconsciously, I knew this. As someone who at various points in her life identified as a writer, I knew that "school" writing did not quite match the "real" writing I did outside of school. When my students groaned or rolled their eyes at my insistence that they spend

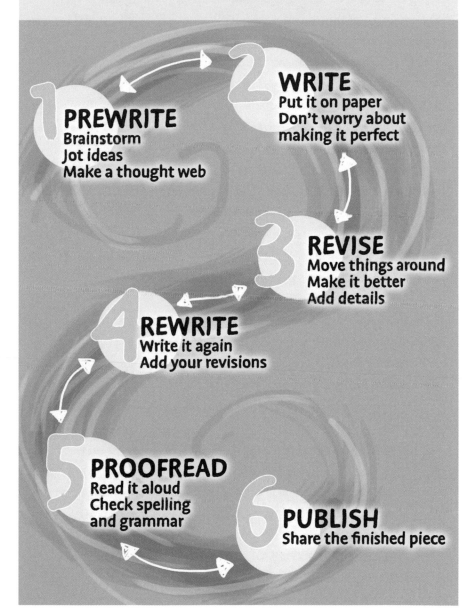

FIGURE 2.2

The writing process with an added sixth step

a specified amount of time working in each stage of the writing process, I felt those reactions in my gut because I *empathized* with them. Being made to march through those steps in a fixed, linear fashion, while helpful to some students, felt overwhelmingly artificial for the majority of my writers.

Where had this idea about writers following a specific, linear process—what Katie Wood Ray describes as "mov[ing] from one piece of writing to the next, faithfully taking each one down the line" (Ray and Laminack 2001, 4)—come from? Most writing workshop devotees would point to Don Murray and Don Graves as the "fathers" of the writing workshop approach, within which a "process approach" to writing is encouraged. But upon closer examination of what both Murray and Graves mean by "process approach," nowhere could I find a suggestion that teachers teach writing process in a standardized fashion. In fact, in his book *Writing: Teachers & Children at Work*, Graves warns his readers of this potential pitfall. He writes,

> *Don't be fooled by the order in which I describe the writing process. I have to use words, which follow each other in systematic and conventional fashion, for you to understand what I am about. This suggests that thoughts follow in systematic order for everyone. Not so. (Graves 2003, 220–221)*

He goes on to say,

> *When a person writes, so many components go into action simultaneously that words fail to portray the real picture. . . . Though the order is unpredictable, what is involved in the writing process can be described. (221)*

In other words, this whole concept of "the" writing process and its poster-worthy iterations? It is, for the most part, a myth.

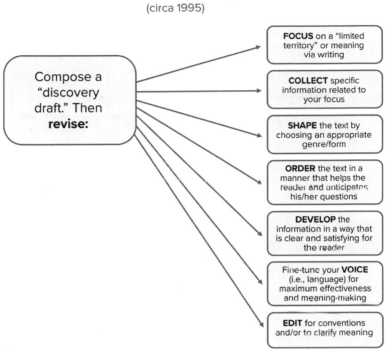

Donald Murray's Writing Process
(circa 1995)

Compose a "discovery draft." Then **revise:**

FOCUS on a "limited territory" or meaning via writing

COLLECT specific information related to your focus

SHAPE the text by choosing an appropriate genre/form

ORDER the text in a manner that helps the reader and anticipates his/her questions

DEVELOP the information in a way that is clear and satisfying for the reader

Fine-tune your **VOICE** (i.e., language) for maximum effectiveness and meaning-making

EDIT for conventions and/or to clarify meaning

FIGURE 2.3
The writing process, as envisioned by Murray in 1995

In his seminal essay "Teaching Writing as a Process Not Product," Murray asserts that there are actually *three*, not five, particular stages of writing (prewriting, writing, and rewriting) and that "the amount of time a writer spends in each stage depends on his personality, his work habits, his maturity as a craftsman, and the challenge of what he is trying to say" (Murray 2009, 2). He goes on to write that "it is not a rigid lock-step process, but *most* writers *most of the time* pass through these three stages" (2; italics mine). In *A Writer Teaches Writing*, Murray goes so far as to admit that the models of writing process that he developed over his life and career (see Figures 2.3 and 2.4 for examples) were mere "guesses," sometimes contradictory ones, that were developed under the "illusion" that he could "make writing easy" for his students (Murray 2003).

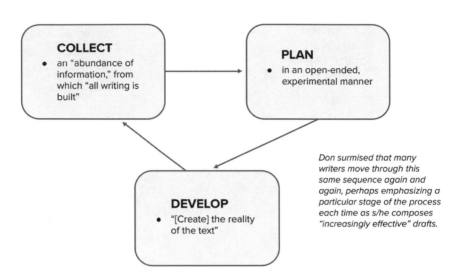

Donald Murray's Writing Process
(circa 2003)

COLLECT
- an "abundance of information," from which "all writing is built"

PLAN
- in an open-ended, experimental manner

DEVELOP
- "[Create] the reality of the text"

Don surmised that many writers move through this same sequence again and again, perhaps emphasizing a particular stage of the process each time as s/he composes "increasingly effective" drafts.

FIGURE 2.4
The writing process, as envisioned by Murray in 2003

To put it simply, both of the "fathers" of the workshop approach to teaching writing, along with Ray and a slew of others, dismiss the idea that writing follows a systematic series of steps, despite what many of us have been led to believe. Instead, they assert that the process writers move through as they compose is unpredictable and dependent on the individual writer—in short, is anything *but* conventional. Yet even as we continue to invoke the work and teachings of mentors like Graves, Murray, and Ray, we fail to match our practice to it, telling students a much *different* story about writing process.

So, where does that leave us? More important, where does it leave our student writers?

Revising How We Teach Writing Process

If we are willing to acknowledge the dynamic nature and the fluidity of writing process, then without question, our teaching—and the "stories" we inadvertently tell our students about writing—must reflect this. This doesn't mean that we must succumb to *Lord of the Flies*-style chaos. What it does mean is that instead of imposing a rigid process structure on our student writers, we can help them—in an organized, even systematic way—envision a variety of *possibilities* for writing process. We can do this by 1) being transparent about our own writing processes, 2) encouraging students to reflect and share their processes, and 3) examining the processes of our most beloved published authors.

SHARING OUR OWN PROCESSES AS WRITERS

By opening a window into our own processes as writers, we can help students envision possibilities for their own writing. (I realize that by including this suggestion here I am also making a giant assumption about teachers engaging in a regular practice of writing; more on this in Chapter 6.) One of the ways I share my own writing processes—which vary depending on the writing task, my mood, and how many cups of coffee I've consumed—is by offering students a peek into my notebooks. Some teacher-writers reserve space in their writing note-books specifically for the kid-friendly writing that they do, to avoid the shameful process of covering up their decidedly *non*-kid-friendly entries. Because I generally do not think that far enough ahead, the notebooks I share with students are littered with sticky notes that I use to shield the little darlings from the darker parts of my psyche—but enough is left bare for them to get the gist of my processes. For example, students are able to see one of the ways I deal with those brain cramps that writers often get when they draft: when I arrive at a point where I can't think of the right word to write, I draw a blank line to "hold"

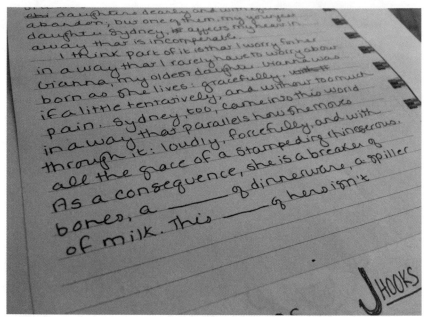

FIGURE 2.5
A blank line holds a place for the right word.

a place for it on the page (see Figure 2.5). This simple move prevents me from interrupting the flow of my writing while also providing me with a visual reminder to come back to it later.

By opening up my notebook to students, I can also help them envision a variety of prewriting possibilities that they might employ at any point during their process, such as creating a brainstorming web, sketching out an idea visually, or—as in Figure 2.6—outlining the "anatomy" of a piece that has been partially drafted in order to visualize how to continue without tearing your hair out in exasperation.

If you're sitting there reading this and feeling all sweaty and clammy because you don't actually *have* a writer's notebook to share with students, don't worry—I'll save my good-natured scolding for Chapter 6. For now, consider some other options:

SHARING STUDENTS' OWN PROCESSES

Perhaps even more powerful than sharing our own processes as writers—after all, we teachers are, for the most part, "old," "out of touch," and "boring," are we not?—is encouraging our students to share *their* processes with one another. In her book *Learning from Classmates: Using Students' Writing as Mentor Texts* (2015), Lisa Eickholdt describes the powerful effect that students' providing a window into their own processes (as well as their compositions) has on their classmates' writing. She writes, "When we use our students' writing as mentor texts, we are helping them identify themselves as someone who writes" (Eickholdt 2015, xvi). Even beyond using their *writing* as mentors, positioning our *students themselves* as mentors from whom their classmates can learn about writing process (see Box 2.1)—e.g., how to generate ideas for writing, edit compositions, set up their work spaces, and so on—can encourage the development of students' own identities as writers and help us create a writing workshop curriculum that is organic, dynamic, and student-centered.

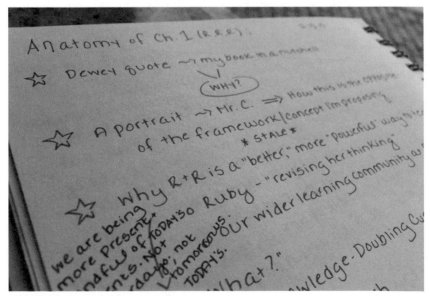

FIGURE 2.6

An "anatomy" outline from my notebook

BOX 2.1 : Writing Process: Students as Mentors

How can we use the varying experiences of our student writers to help us develop and organize a process curriculum in our writing workshop? One way is to devote one or two shares a week specifically to process. For example, we can invite students to answer a process-centered question, such as "What do you do when you are getting a piece ready for a public audience?" or "How do you decide if a composition should be abandoned?" Each time, we might take a few minutes to chart their answers or simply ask students to listen closely and jot down notes about what they hear.

If you'd rather not use your share time to engage in these kinds of process-oriented discussions, consider devoting a series of focus lessons to sharing ideas, asking questions, or collaboratively problem

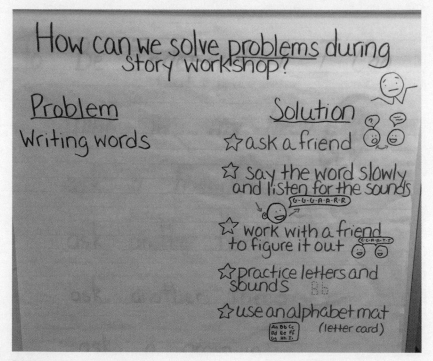

FIGURE 2.7
Charts from Becky Wright's kindergarten classroom

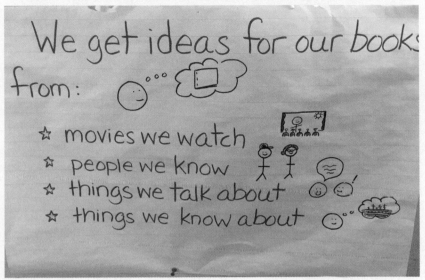

FIGURE 2.8

Charts from Becky Wright's kindergarten classroom

solving some of the challenges related to writing process. In Becky Wright's kindergarten classroom, for instance, we developed a brief focus lesson around some possible ideas for what students might do when they want to write a word they don't yet know by heart. Another lesson was centered around discussing where students might get ideas for the books they were making during story workshop. The charts in Figures 2.7 and 2.8 (and others like them) are considered "living documents" that are revised and added to each time we revisit them and serve as scaffolds for students to use when they are working independently—in other words, when they are actively engaged in the process of writing.

SHARING THE PROCESSES OF OUR FAVORITE AUTHORS & ILLUSTRATORS

Finally, we can help students envision possibilities for writing process by sharing the processes of our most beloved authors and illustrators—what Katie Wood Ray (1999) calls their "office work." (As a process nerd, this is something I live to do when working with students and teachers.) The good news is, you don't have to be an author/illustrator Twitter creeper like me to find out how, for example, Cece Bell blogged about her experience growing up deaf long before she ever sketched a panel of her Newbery Honor–winning illustrations in *El Deafo* (2014), or how Marla Frazee, while developing her idea for *The Farmer and the Clown* (2014), began by sketching the two main characters before creating early (and very rough) thumbnails of the story. (See Box 2.2.)

BOX 2.2: A Peek into the Processes of Cece Bell and Marla Frazee

FIGURE 2.9

Marla: "This is the first drawing I did of the two characters. It kicked off my thinking about what the story could be."

"*El Deafo* actually began as a blog. About seven years ago, I was in the check-out line at the grocery store. My cashier was really hard to lip-read. I couldn't understand *anything* she was saying … she became increasingly agitated with me to the point of anger. I got so flustered and was completely in tears by the time I got to the car. The whole drive home, I replayed that unfortunate interaction over and over, but this time I fantasized about what I should have done and what I should have said. Why didn't I just pull out my hearing aids, shove

---

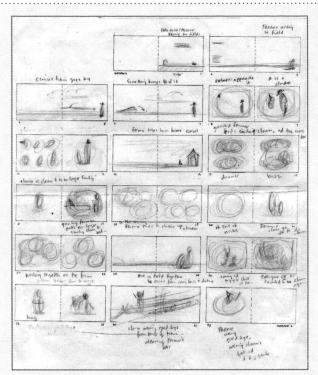

FIGURE 2.10

Marla: "This is one of the many, many, many versions of early thumbnails."

them in the cashier's face, and say, "I can't understand you. I'm deaf. See?" But that's not what I did, because I never did that. I had been deaf for over thirty years and I couldn't say those words – I just couldn't. So I started this blog. And as I wrote it, I discovered I had real stories to tell especially about my childhood."

—Cece Bell (2015)

What you *do* need to be, however, is able to type "[author/illustrator's name] + interview" into Google. Doing so will uncover a veritable gold mine of information that will offer you and your students a window into the composing lives of such authors as Jess Keating (*How to Outrun a Crocodile When Your Shoes Are Untied*), who offers this look into her writing process in a 2016 appearance on librarian Matthew Winner's *Let's Get Busy* podcast:

> *I was walking—kind of hiking in the woods one day doing, you know, whatever I do, and the phrase how to outrun a crocodile when your shoes are untied popped into my head. And . . . I was like, "Well, that's a funny title, isn't it?" and—I think in that moment, the character that I write about, Ana, in that book, she just kind of—you know—formulated in my head, and— boom—everything was there, and I knew everything about her.*

Jess' insight into her process in this interview could become the starting point for a classwide look into how writers get ideas or how a word or phrase can become a "seed idea" for a new composition.

If you *are* on Twitter, all the better, as I can't think of a single author or illustrator who is too busy to respond to a tweet from a teacher (or even more so, a student). (See Box 2.3 for more ideas on how to help your students sneak a look at their favorite authors' or illustrators' processes.)

BOX 2.3: Want to Creep on Your Favorite Authors or Illustrators and Their Processes? Check Out These Helpful Websites & Podcasts

- Seven Impossible Things Before Breakfast (www.blaine.org)
- Reading Rockets Video Interviews (http://www.readingrockets. org/books/interviews)
- Children's Books: Author Q & A (via *The Guardian*) (http:// www.theguardian.com/childrens-books-site/series/childrens- books-author-q-as)
- Scholastic's Index of Authors & Illustrators (http://www. scholastic.com/teacher/ab/biolist.htm)

- HarperCollins' Index of Authors & Illustrators (http://www.harpercollinschildrens.com/Kids/AuthorsAndIllustrators/Browse.aspx)
- *Sharpread* (blog) (https://sharpread.wordpress.com)
- *The Yarn* (podcast) (https://itunes.apple.com/us/podcast/the-yarn/id1028877816?mt=2)
- *Let's Get Busy* (podcast) (http://lgbpodcast.blogspot.com)

Renewing Our Process-Oriented Curriculum

Despite the false narratives about writing process that continue to be shared across classrooms, in teacher supply stores, and on Pinterest, our own experiences as writers, the experiences of our diverse population of student writers, and the experiences of the authors and illustrators we love most hold true to the notion that there is no "one" way to move a composition from idea to publication (if it even gets that far). Rather, writers use multiple processes—even across different compositions!—to develop an idea and nurture it to the point of wanting to share it with a wider audience.

By charting, mapping, and discussing in detail these multiple processes, which open a world of possibility for our student writers, we can simultaneously open up a world of *teaching* writing process and, through daily or weekly collaboration with our students, build a process-oriented writing curriculum that is authentically based, boundless in scope, and renewable year after year.

*Daily practice with images both written and drawn is
rare once we have lost our baby teeth ... a certain state
of mind is also lost. A certain capacity of the mind is
shuttered and for most people, it stays that way for life.*

—Lynda Barry

CHAPTER 3

Renew What It Means to "Write"

Day One of the new school year also meant that it was Day One of writer's workshop in Becky Wright's kindergarten classroom at Rollinsford Grade School in Rollinsford, New Hampshire. Becky had just read Marla Frazee's *The Boss Baby* (2010) to her group of eighteen fresh-faced five-year-olds, had given them a brief "materials" tour, and had asked them to make their first important decision as writers in kindergarten: whether they wanted the first book they wrote to go the "long way," as *The Boss Baby* is oriented, or the "tall way," as such familiar books as Mac Barnett and Jon Klassen's *Sam and Dave Dig a Hole* and almost all Dr. Seuss books are oriented.

Only one student, P., voiced a concern that he didn't "know how" to write a book. The rest of his classmates happily dove into their writing, composing books about themselves, their families, their friends, and—in about half a dozen cases—rainbows.

After reassuring P. that he *did* in fact know how to write a book, and that if he was absolutely convinced otherwise, he could *pretend* to know how, Becky and I wandered over to the students with whom we would conduct our first conferring sessions of the school year. As Becky headed over to one of the writers of a "rainbow" book, I wove my way over to Lucas, a towheaded, wide-eyed four-year-old whose rounded cheeks had captured my heart the second I'd laid eyes on him earlier that morning.

"Hi Lucas," I greeted him, carefully lowering myself into a tiny chair with all the grace of Godzilla. "What book are you writing today?" Then I saw it: a page full of what appeared to be blue-markered scribbles accompanied by two distinct, square-shaped blobs. I cleared my throat and began to sweat profusely, wondering what in heaven's name I was going to confer with him about. *What is there to ask about scribbles?* I thought to myself. *Shoulda picked a rainbow kid.*

Those of you who are accustomed to working with our youngest writers are likely horrified by my reaction. You should be! It was only my second year as a literacy specialist, and I had spent the majority of my first year avoiding the group of students with whom I had the least amount of experience. I didn't yet understand the richness and the complexity of many young writers' compositions. But that was about to change.

What I discovered from listening to Lucas tell me about his book was that what looked like scribbles were in fact elements of an elaborately composed visual story. In fact, what Lucas had composed that afternoon was a retelling of the scene in the original *Star Wars* movie where Obi-Wan Kenobi and Darth Vader battle it out with lightsabers before Obi-Wan sacrifices himself for the sake of his friends by allowing Vader to strike him down.

I was astonished. By most laypeople's—and let's face it, some educators'—accounts, Lucas was not yet a "writer." And yet here he was, composing a complex retelling of a story on the first day of kindergarten!

I should have been far less astonished than I was. It has, after all, been long established that young children create meaningful text through a variety of ways before they ever write a single letter. In their book *Kidwatching: Documenting Children's Literacy Development* (2002), Gretchen Owocki and Yetta Goodman point out that "meaning is made as children weave together writing [i.e., printed text] with talk, drawing, movement, and sound" (86). Just recently, though, I had also begun to think more broadly about composition—not just for our youngest writers, but for all writers—as a result of an epiphany I'd had while sitting in my physician's waiting room.

Out of boredom, I had opened the Facebook app on my iPhone, hoping to peruse my news feed and read my friends' status updates. Unfortunately, because my phone was one of the more outdated models at the time, all I could see on my screen were unloaded images, some of which were accompanied by a small amount of written text.

As I shook my iPhone in an unsuccessful (and completely foolish) attempt to shock it into loading all of those images, I realized something: Facebook—and the way my friends told "stories" about their daily lives—had irrevocably changed. Whereas just a year ago my news feed was largely composed of text-based status updates (e.g., "Grabbing some lunch with my better half at Chipotle!"), for the past several months, my friends, more than ever before, were *using images to digitally journal their lives.*

Why was this such a light-bulb moment? Because in my own classroom, and in the classrooms of most literacy teachers with whom I'd worked over the past decade, this way of journaling our lives, of telling our stories, was not reflected in the writing we were inviting students to do. The older students get, the less likely they are to see and hear a picture book read aloud, making it unlikely for them to look to these authors and illustrators as mentors for their own writing. In fact, visual composition is often seen as a distraction; one of the most frequent remarks I hear from teachers about the "reluctant writers" in their classrooms is that all they ever want to do is draw pictures.

Rethinking What It Means to "Write"

In 2006, Sarah E. Rose, Richard P. Jolley, and Esther Burkitt, researchers from three separate universities in the United Kingdom, conducted a review of the "attitudes and practices of teachers, parents, and children themselves" regarding children's drawing experience over the course of their school careers. They found that not only does the amount of time during which children engage in visual composition decrease over time (beginning shortly after children begin formal schooling), but also that "drawing is given little importance by [educators] ... who simply see it as a way to keep children occupied, out of mischief, and as a means of decorating the classroom walls" (343).

In their book *Talking, Drawing, and Writing: Lessons for Our Youngest Writers* (2007), Martha Horn and Mary Ellen Giacobbe, two teachers with over sixty years' experience between them, humbly confess their own outdated views of drawing. They write, "although we had always honored and valued drawing as a way of expressing oneself, we had never quite honored and valued it the same as the written word." In their book, they convincingly lay out six reasons why drawing is important for young writers (which I expand to include students of *all* ages in Table 3.1). Drawing, they conclude, is a medium through which students can potentially develop language or tell a story *as* deeply, if not *more* deeply, than they can using only written text.

TABLE 3.1

Six Reasons Why Visual Composition Matters—For Students of ALL Ages

WHAT HORN & GIACOBBE SAY IN RELATION TO YOUNG WRITERS	HOW THIS RELATES TO WRITERS OF ALL AGES
"Drawing is one . . . way that beginning writers represent and understand meaning" (61).	When approaching an understanding of any new concept—the transmission of sounds through sound waves, for example—learners of all ages are frequently able to represent meaning *visually* (i.e., using symbols, illustrations, or gestures) long before they are able to do so using content-specific vocabulary.
"Drawing is a way for children to be heard" (61).	It has often been said that writing is a way for us to be heard, a vehicle through which we may tell our collective and individual stories. Who could argue with the idea that we can be heard just as effectively through visual composition? (Just check your favorite social media feed for proof of how this notion transcends age!)
"Drawing is a medium through which children can develop language" (62).	While this has most certainly been proven true for our youngest writers, it has also become a way to effectively engage students of all ages for whom English is a second language—as well as for those students who are struggling academically.
"Drawing allows children to go deeper into their stories" (62).	A 2011 study by Noella Mackenzie of Australia's Charles Sturt University concludes that teachers who teach their youngest students to "see drawing and writing as a unified system for making meaning" unambiguously develop writers whose texts "are more complex than those they can create with words alone" (322). This conclusion can refer to writers of all ages.
"Through drawing, children [can learn] about the craft of writing" (63).	In her book *In Pictures and In Words: Teaching the Qualities of Good Writing Through Illustration Study*, Katie Wood Ray argues that "children learning an illustration technique are also learning a way of representing meaning that they could just as well do with words, in a different sort of text" (2010, 15–16). For example, students could study ways of representing perspective through illustration that can be transferred to how writers represent perspective through text.
"Drawing . . . is what young children do naturally and playfully" (64).	Opportunities for play shouldn't wane just because we get older. In fact, the older we get, the more responsibilities we have, and the more we should *embrace* opportunities for play. Just look at the explosion in popularity of sketchnoting and Zentangle tutorials on YouTube for evidence of how this need for "play" can translate into opportunities for visual composition and design!

In an article titled "Drawing to Learn in Science" (2011), researchers Shaaron Ainsworth, Vaughn Prain, and Russell Tytler assert that "student drawing should be explicitly recognized alongside writing, reading, and talking as a key element in science education" (1096) due to its ability to deepen students' understanding along with their ability to reason, to organize and integrate both new and existing knowledge, and to communicate or clarify key concepts and ideas. In other words, visual composition helps students to *think* and to *write*—and should be valued as much, if not more, than more traditional forms of "writing."

Most illustrators also make the case for why visual composition is important and should be valued more than it traditionally has been. Debbie Ridpath Ohi, author and/or illustrator of such beloved titles as *Where Are My Books?*, *I'm Bored*, and a variety of reissued novels written by author Judy Blume, had this to say in an e-mail:

> *Sketching visual ideas is an ESSENTIAL part of my process when I am writing . . . not just with picture books but also with the middle-grade novel I am working on. Drawing helps me flesh out characters as well as [work] out scenes and action sequences. I also find that drawing is a wonderful way of generating new story ideas.*

In an essay titled "Words and Pictures, an Intimate Distance" (2010), author and illustrator Shaun Tan (*Rules of Summer*, *The Arrival*) says this about visual composition:

> *I find it difficult to talk about the "language" of drawing, of lines, shapes, colors, and contrasts, because it does not translate very well into words. However, it is generally guided by a fairly simple question, regardless of whether I am drawing a tree from my window or an imaginary creature; "does it feel true to experience?" That is, does it have an equivalent balance of clarity and mystery, definition and openness that shapes our experience of the real world: a sense that [the reader] grasp some things, but not everything, that there is always something elusive in every honest description.*

Whether we are discussing personal narratives, poetry, fictional stories, or informational texts, the "simple question" that Tan refers to extends to the composing opportunities we offer students: Do they feel "true to experience"? With visual composition becoming ever more ubiquitous in our world *outside* of school—as demonstrated by our use of emojis, memes, and storytelling applications such as Instagram and Snapchat, as well as by the ever-increasing popularity of comics and graphic novels—wouldn't it make sense to collectively broaden our idea of what it means to "write" *within* school?

Revising How We Define—and Teach—"Writing"

In Emily Spear and Sheryl Horton's first- and second-grade multiage classroom, students are engaged in a true writer's workshop experience. *What* they write, *how* they choose to write, and *for whom* they write are all decisions that the students, not the teachers, make on a daily basis.

Camden, a second grader, has chosen to write a comic called *The Awesome Adventure* (see Figure 3.1). As I confer with Camden, I am immediately struck by how well he understands his powerful position as the author and illustrator of his piece. He is able to explain, with great confidence, its complex plot, the wide variety of composing decisions he has made as an illustrator, and how he intends to continue to develop the story over the course of the next several days.

By contrast, let's look at one of the pieces Camden composed largely through writing: a book about Minecraft (see Figure 3.2). In this composition, Camden has made a variety of intentional composing decisions, just as he did with *The Awesome Adventure*. For example, we can see that with the inclusion of the page titled "All About Blocks," Camden has decided to divide this informational text into different sections. Camden has also decided to maintain consistency in his written text, as evidenced by the repetition of the phrase "you can" on more than one page. There is also consistency in the layout, with

FIGURE 3.1

Page from Camden's *The Awesome Adventure*

a line of text at the top of each page and a matching illustration at the bottom of the page.

Let's consider for a moment which of Camden's compositions would be more valued in most primary-grade classrooms. If we are being completely honest, we would agree that the Minecraft book would likely receive the most accolades, with its clear sense of genre, its organizational consistency, and—most of all—its inclusion of more written text. Can we rightfully argue, though, that this piece is, page by page, more compositionally complex than *The Awesome Adventure*? I would argue that we cannot. Yet time and time again, I have heard the concerns of teachers (Camden's present teachers excluded) whose students compose pieces that more closely resemble *The Awesome Adventure* than the Minecraft book—and these concerns often take the form of "the students aren't *writing* enough."

What, exactly, does this mean? When teachers bemoan the fact that their students aren't *writing* enough, they are almost always referring to the act of putting words to paper (or to screen)—the sort

FIGURE 3.2
Excerpt from
Camden's
Minecraft book

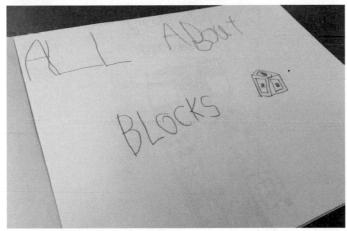

Quote Mash-Up

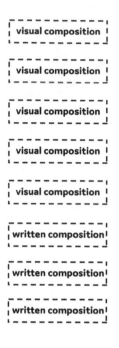

"I find that good [work] requires conscientious effort: active research, careful observation of things around me, ongoing experimentation and reference-gathering, all of which exist 'behind the scenes' .... [Composers] need to work hard to make sure their creative soil is well tilled and fertilized. They need to look outward and actively accumulate a swag of influences, things to bring along when taking that line for a walk."

"Maybe some [composers] enjoy the first draft—the part of the [composing] process when anything is possible, and you're out there forging your own path. I hate that part....First drafts always make me feel anxious and a little desperate—like, 'Oh God, I just need to get all of this out and on paper, so that I have something to work with.'"

"I look for the spaces [in my work]... where I can add detail, give weight to some event, reinforce humor, wink obliquely, allow for a...pause, and—most importantly—deepen the emotional moments."

"... the first time you try to do something, you will probably fail. This goes for trying to swim and trying to [compose]. The thing to do is to see the first draft as the shallow end of the pool. Keep practicing and you'll get to the deep end eventually."

"I like showing the [rough drafts] to people and seeing where I cringe or feel the need to explain or defend something in them, because then you know where your trouble spots are. "

"My favorite thing is coming up with the ideas. I spend months, even years, having conversations with myself, playing out scenarios in my head, getting to know the characters before I [compose] one thing.... I really enjoy that process."

" ...my work doesn't start off looking anything like the finished product. In fact, [the work is] downright horrible at first. But...if I keep re-working it and do it again and again and again...eventually I am able to create something that I am pleased with."

"I think too many children get frustrated if [a composition] doesn't come out the way they want it to on the first go, so they give up or they don't [compose] at all. I try to show that, like them, I don't get it right the first time either. I don't get it right on the second time, or the third, or fourth. But each time I get a little closer and the more I do it, the better it gets."

visual composition

visual composition

visual composition

visual composition

visual composition

written composition

written composition

written composition

FIGURE 3.3

Some of our favorite author quotes

of writing you are reading here. But I would argue that this concept of "writing" unnecessarily—and inauthentically—compartmentalizes what is, outside the realm of school, a much broader set of processes, experiences, and products. In fact, when we broaden our notions of what "writing" is to include not just written composition but visual composition, we can see that there are more similarities than differences in the two processes.

To demonstrate, let's play a game. In Figure 3.3 you will find a set of quotes that have been excerpted directly from interviews with some of my (and my students') favorite authors and illustrators. To play the game, read the quotes carefully and see if you can match the *kind* of composing these authors and illustrators are referring to—written or visual—to the quote. Identifying words or phrases have been modified. Ready? Go!

If you guessed correctly, your answers would be: *visual, written, visual, written, visual, written, visual,* and *visual.* (Who these quotes are from, and where the interviews occurred, can be found in Box 3.3 at the end of this chapter.) How did you do? Were you able to distinguish the quotes about visual composition from the ones about writing? If so, what were the clues that led you to the correct answers? If not, what tripped you up?

Having asked a number of colleagues and Twitter friends to humor me by playing this game—only *one* of whom chose the correct answers 100 percent of the time—I can say with all confidence that accurately identifying which quotes refer to which type of composition is, at best, a crap shoot. This is because *there is little difference between the two.* Both kinds of composition require (or are significantly enhanced by) active research, careful observation, and experimentation; both involve drafting, revising, and generating ideas; both, if the author or artist is lucky (and persistent), lead to finished products; and both necessitate the constant tilling of one's creative soil. In short, as Horn and Giacobbe assert in their book, "Drawing is not rehearsal for writing: drawing *is* writing" (3). Why, then, does one kind of composing continue to be valued—and taught—far more than the other?

Let's pretend that I've convinced you by now to join me in broadening our collective idea of what it means to "write"—even beyond incorporating visual composition into our classrooms (see Box 3.1). I hope you understand that I am not suggesting that we throw the proverbial baby out with the bathwater (as we educators are wont to do; see our actions within the last several decades in regard to reading instruction, inquiry, and project-based learning). Rather, I am suggesting that

- we *open up a much larger world of possibilities for student writers* than has traditionally been made available;

- we *practice new ways of "seeing" composition* as well as the myriad of purposeful decisions that are made by those who compose for a particular audience; and

- we *honor the wide range of composition types*, especially those that feel much more "true to experience" than the ones that are typically offered in school.

Even if I *have* convinced you, some of you may be panicking right now. You may be thinking, "I already have too much on my plate when it comes to teaching writing! How can I possibly add *more*?" (Some of you may even be in the process of drafting an alarmed tweet to me at this very moment. Hold off for a quick second!)

BOX 3.1 : "Remixing" as Composition

Perhaps you're warming to the idea of broadening our collective idea about writing to include visual composition. Hooray! Ready to push the envelope further? Consider the idea of *remixing*. You may have heard of a "remix" or a "mashup" as it pertains to music. But what is remixing in terms of writing composition? Kevin Hodgson, a sixth-grade teacher, musician, and blogger, regularly engages in remixing both at home and with his students. One of the many ways he does this is by using the online code editor Thimble to remix poetry, campaign posters, memes, and more. One of my favorites among the

---

remixes he's highlighted on his blog involves the blending together of audio and video clips from LEGO ads to highlight the different ways we market toys to children of different genders. His full post, as well as a link to the LEGO mashup, can be found here: https://dogtrax. edublogs.org/2012/12/06/remixing-lego-advertisements-and-considering-gender-stereotypes/.

Kitri Doherty, a teacher at this same school, has engaged her fifth- and sixth-grade students in an inquiry involving remixing. For example, Lauren and her classmate Ruby have remixed a poem about basketball by creating a digital version of the poem that incorporates video, spoken-word audio, text, and music to create a new, original composition. Charlie, who typically produces very little content during writer's workshop, has remixed an Eminem song by pairing isolated lyrics with a "chill trap mix" called "Sensations" by the artist Fluidified, giving the song a fuller, more mystical feel. Madison has attempted to transform a favorite picture book, *Edward the Emu*, into a collage that captures the essence of the story as a whole. Although these students are in all instances using previously composed pieces of content, no one can argue that they are not also composing new material or making important composition decisions regarding modality, format, organization, tone, and much, much more.

Renewing Our Practice—As Well as Our Curriculum

Exploring more visual composition needn't add anything "extra" to an already overstuffed writing curriculum. Instead of focusing our efforts on trying to teach our student writers the overwhelming variety of compositional forms, purposes, and modalities that exist in the world—an exercise in futility, at best—I would suggest that we focus on teaching students how to "read like a writer" (see Box 3.2) so that they may develop the capacity to *independently* analyze, emulate, and ultimately compose in a wide variety of genres, forms, and styles. Because really: how can we possibly teach our students *the entire range of writing that exists in the world* without making some very tough (and arguably political) decisions about which genres, forms, and styles to include or exclude? By targeting our efforts on helping students learn how to read like writers, and using their input to build a comprehensive yet student-responsive writing curriculum, we are giving our students the gift of being able to sustain a composing life beyond our classrooms. And isn't that, ultimately, what we want to do?

BOX 3.2: What Does It Mean to "Read Like a Writer"?

We read texts for a variety of reasons: to entertain ourselves, to gather information about an issue or topic, to understand a perspective other than our own (or, perhaps, to reaffirm our own values and beliefs). As writers, we can also "read" a variety of texts in ways that can ultimately, as Ralph Fletcher has pointed out, "lift and inform and infuse" our own writing. In her book *Wondrous Words* (1999), Katie Wood Ray likens this kind of reading to "how any craftsperson would study the techniques of others who practice the same craft" (12)—by, among other things, noticing, naming, and envisioning using it in her own work.

Teaching our students how to do this important work empowers them in ways that extend beyond our classroom—and it can happen with any genre, form, modality, or topic (even those we have not yet imagined)! For example, reading a variety of picture books through the lens of a writer can help our students build an enormous repertoire of *purposes* for writing, of *formats* or *layouts* they might use in their work, of *craft techniques* they might experiment with, and of *text features* they might use. The same goes for any form or genre we choose to read "like a writer," leading to a much more sustainable body of knowledge that will continue to benefit our students as writers and illustrators for the rest of their lives.

For more about teaching students to read like a writer, which has been much more articulately explained in numerous books on the topic, check out the following resources:

Dorfman, Lynn, and Rose Capelli. 2009. *Mentor Texts: Teaching Writing Through Children's Literature, K–6.* Portland, ME: Stenhouse.

Fletcher, Ralph, and JoAnn Portalupi. 1998. *Craft Lessons: Teaching Writing, K–8.* Portland, ME: Stenhouse.

Gallagher, Kelly. 2011. *Write Like This: Teaching Real-World Writing Through Modeling and Mentor Texts.* Portland, ME: Stenhouse.

Marchetti, Allison, and Rebekah O'Dell. 2015. *Writing with Mentors: How to Reach Every Writer in the Room Using Current, Engaging Mentor Texts.* Portsmouth, NH: Heinemann.

Ray, Katie Wood. 2010. *In Pictures and In Words: Teaching the Qualities of Good Writing Through Illustration Study.* Portsmouth, NH: Heinemann.

Shubitz, Stacey. 2016. *Craft Moves: Lesson Sets for Teaching Writing with Mentor Texts.* Portland, ME: Stenhouse.

Broadening our ideas about what writing "is" can be scary, as if we are opening up a Pandora's box. But in all reality, continuing to teach our student writers through a narrow, outdated lens—one that, in overvaluing written composition, does not accurately tell a story about the world of writing beyond most schools and classrooms—harms their development as writers by limiting the kinds of composing they are exposed to and encouraged to practice. As Donald Graves wrote in his influential 1984 essay "The Enemy Is Orthodoxy," while long-held traditions in the teaching of writing may be "necessary for temporary sanity" that we can use to develop the coping mechanisms we need to navigate the complex world of teaching, such orthodoxies also "prevent us from being sensitive to writers" (Newkirk and Kittle 2013, 215). Alternatively, embracing a more expansive view of writing can ensure that students' experiences within our classrooms feel much more "true" to their real-life experiences outside the classroom.

And besides—isn't sanity overrated?

BOX 3.3: Quotes and Their Sources from Figure 3.3

Shaun Tan (2013):
"I find that good [drawing] requires conscientious effort: active research, careful observation of things around me, ongoing experimentation and reference-gathering, all of which exist 'behind the scenes.' . . . [Artists] need to work hard to make sure their creative soil is well tilled and fertilized. They need to look outward and actively accumulate a swag of influences, things to bring along when taking that line for a walk.'" (Introduction)

Marla Frazee (Danielson 2014):
"I look for the spaces [in my work] . . . where I can add detail, give weight to some event, reinforce humor, wink obliquely, allow for a . . . pause, and—most importantly—deepen the emotional moments."

Jon Klassen (Danielson 2011a):
"I like showing the [rough drafts] to people and seeing where I cringe or feel the need to explain or defend something in them, because then you know where your trouble spots are."

Rainbow Rowell (n.d.):
"Maybe some [writers] enjoy the first draft—the part of the [writing] process when anything is possible, and you're out there forging your own path. I hate that part. All I can think about when I'm starting a [book] are all the [words I haven't written] yet. I

---

actually feel them, hanging around my neck, tugging at me. First drafts always make me feel anxious and a little desperate—like, 'Oh God, I just need to get all of this out and on paper, so that I have something to work with.'"

Kwame Alexander (2016):
"My favorite thing is coming up with the ideas. I spend months, even years, having conversations with myself, playing out scenarios in my head, getting to know the characters before I [write] one thing down. I really enjoy that process."

Jenni Holm (Sharp 2013):
"The first time you try to do something, you will probably fail. This goes for trying to swim and trying to [write]. The thing to do is to see the first draft as the shallow end of the pool. Keep practicing and you'll get to the deep end eventually."

John Rocco (Danielson 2011b):
"My work doesn't start off looking anything like the finished product. In fact, [the drawings are] downright horrible at first. [So is the writing.] But ... if I keep reworking it and do it again and again and again ... eventually I am able to create something that I am pleased with.

" I think too many children get frustrated if [a drawing] doesn't come out the way they want it to on the first go, so they give up or they don't [draw] at all. I try to show that, like them, I don't get it right the first time either. I don't get it right on the second time, or the third, or fourth. But each time I get a little closer and the more I do it, the better it gets."

Pinterest is not pedagogy.

—Donalyn Miller

. . . .

CHAPTER 4

Renew the Tools We Use to Teach Our Student Writers

My husband David and I have long attempted to get our daughters to help out around the house by using approximately 378 different iterations of the ubiquitous "chore chart." From wooden charts that come packaged with a slew colorful magnets to laminated schedules we created ourselves using Microsoft Word, we have tried nearly everything. Despite the embarrassing number of chore charts I have pinned to my Pinterest boards, none of them have seemed to help our children become more mindful of their surroundings—at least, not in any meaningful, sustainable way. We still spend close to 20 percent of our waking hours asking the kids to unload the dishwasher, take out the recycling, pick up their shoes, start a load of laundry—the list goes on.

They're not bad kids, nor is it that they *want* us to nag them on a daily basis. But the chores my husband and I ask our daughters to do simply aren't meaningful to them; they are quite happy to climb into an unmade bed at the end of a long day or grab a pair of socks from behind a kitchen stool. In fact, until recently, the tools my husband and I used to promote more independence around the house have actually worked *against* our goal!

As is my habit, this failure of parenting has caused me to reflect on my work as an educator—specifically, on the tools I have used over the years to teach my student writers. Graphic organizers, story starters, revising checklists—these tools can be found in almost every classroom where students spend regular, sustained chunks of time composing text. They can be found on paper, online, and organized in colorful, laminated binders. Type "writing tools" into Pinterest's search box and you'll find an endless supply of tools that teachers can use to teach their student writers—many of which link to *more than 400* that you can purchase for a nominal fee on the popular online marketplace Teachers Pay Teachers. There are tools for teaching students to organize their writing, to generate ideas, to vary their sentence structure—even to develop "emoji stories" (one of my personal favorite pastimes).

If you want a tool for teaching your student writers, you can find it just about anywhere, anytime and use it in your classroom—with minimal effort.

And many teachers do. But at what cost?

Rethinking the Tools We Use to Teach Our Student Writers

In their book *DIY Literacy: Teaching Tools for Differentiation, Rigor, and Independence*, Kate Roberts and Maggie Beattie Roberts soundly claim that the appropriate tools can "help students work harder, smarter, and on their own" (2016, 2). They urge teachers to rethink tools and their uses in order to more effectively help students retain information and to personalize them to fit students' particular needs. They write,

> Tools have always helped us reach farther than our bodies and minds allow us to alone.
>   We have always needed a little bit of help to get to where we want to go. . . . As educators and students, we are no different. Sometimes we can reach our dreams; we just need some help to do it. (2–3)

What could be more true than that? Tools *are* helpful. For writers who struggle in particular, tools can "level the playing field" by taking away some of the balls that writers are simultaneously juggling in the air each time they sit down to compose (see Figure 4.1).

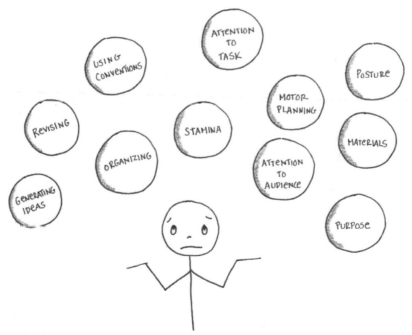

FIGURE 4.1
Modified from a graphic developed by Gretchen Hanser, MS, OTR (2001)

Unfortunately, some of the more common tools we use in our class-rooms—many of which are created *apart from students* and *without their input*—can also send students messages about writing (and about themselves as writers) that, like the tools my husband and I used with our daughters, actually work against their goals (see Table 4.1).

TABLE 4.1
The Tools We Use in Classrooms—and the Potential (if Unintended) Messages
They Send

TOOL USED IN MANY CLASSROOMS	MESSAGE THIS TOOL CAN POTENTIALLY SEND ABOUT WRITING OR WRITERS
Graphic organizer	*There is one way, and only one way, for you to write this.* OR *All [personal narratives, persuasive essays, etc.] are written in precisely this manner—or at least in a highly predictable one.*
Revision checklist	*Attending to these items, and only these items, is important because they are on this checklist.* OR *Attending to these items alone will make your writing better.*
Story starter or writing prompt	*Writers must rely on others to help them generate ideas for writing.*
Preformatted writing paper (e.g., lined paper) or digital template	*You cannot be trusted to make intentional, meaningful decisions about the organization or layout of your composition.*
"Words to use instead of" display	*Using these words in your writing is always superior to not using them.*
"Writing process" display	*There is only one way for writers to move through the process of writing.*
Writing rubric	*Evaluating writing has less to do with the relationship between the text and the reader and more to do with these fixed elements.*

In addition, predeveloped tools like those we find on Pinterest and Teachers Pay Teachers are the product of *teacher* thinking, not *student* thinking, which severely limits the learning that students could be doing. Instead of students doing the "heavy lifting" of developing appropriate tools for themselves, we are doing it for them. So how do we offer student writers ways of developing appropriate tools that are simultaneously 1) responsive to their particular needs as writers, 2) empowering rather than enabling, and 3) sustainable in the long term?

Revising the Tools We Use to Teach Our Student Writers

It would be foolish to ask someone who wants to nail two pieces of wood together to use anything other than a hammer—a tool that has been around for millions of years and is clearly the most appropriate for this pretty basic task. Well, did you know there exist approximately *two dozen types of hammers* (see Figure 4.2), each suited to a particular job? (It's true—I engaged in a ridiculous amount of research so I could use this metaphor.) Despite the straightforward nature of nailing two pieces of wood together, someone who wishes to do so must understand enough about tools to know which hammer to select. For example,

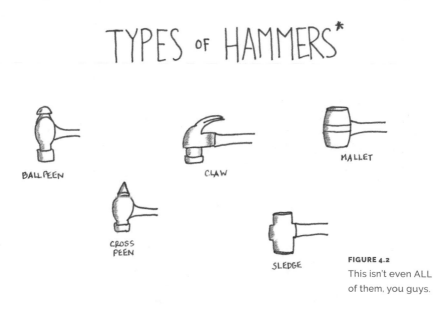

TYPES OF HAMMERS*

BALL PEEN

CLAW

MALLET

CROSS PEEN

SLEDGE

FIGURE 4.2
This isn't even ALL of them, you guys.

*ACCORDING TO MY (ADMITTEDLY LIMITED) RESEARCH

one would never use a tack hammer when building a bookcase. (Trust me on this.) If we simply offered a person the appropriate hammer to use *for this particular task*, would he or she necessarily know which one to use the next time, for the next task—especially if it required working with an entirely different type of wood?

Not necessarily—unless, somehow, through the power of osmosis, the person were able to figure out *why* the hammer offered was the right one for the job. Even if we revealed the reason, there's still no guarantee that he or she would be able to choose the right hammer the next time.

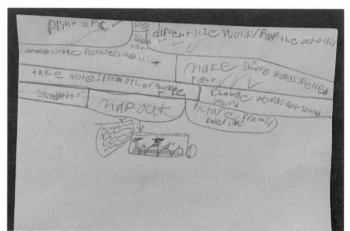

FIGURE 4.3
Zoe's revising checklist

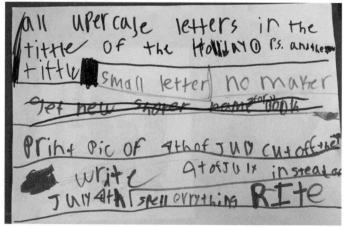

FIGURE 4.4
Adele's revising checklist

Teaching writing is considerably less straightforward than teaching someone to nail two pieces of wood together (no disrespect to carpenters). So, instead of offering our students a tool to use—or even a selection of tools to use in the name of "differentiation"—for every compositional task, why not empower them to create their *own* tools? Doing so may take considerably more time—although one could argue that it takes just as much time to teach them how to use existing tools. Teaching students *how to create their own revising checklists*—like the ones two second-grade writers, Adele and Zoe, created during their writing workshop (see Figures 4.3 and 4.4)—can eliminate the need to continually teach students how to use scores of such checklists, none of which are guaranteed to meet each writer's particular needs.

What did Adele and Zoe's teachers do to teach them how to create these revising plans? In essence, they used a combination of whole-class discussion, peer conferencing, and individual conferring to help both them—as well as their classmates—consider what they could do to make their writing better (and how to keep track of these ideas). During whole-class discussions, they shared how professional writers such as Eric Carle (*The Very Hungry Caterpillar*) and Wendy Anderson Halperin (*Peace*) revise their work and asked carefully crafted questions to help students consider ways that *they* might engage in this process. Some of the questions the teachers asked include:

- What do you notice about what these writers do to get ready to revise their work?

- How might you revise (add, subtract, move, or change) your work to make it more compelling for your readers?

- What might you do to keep track of your revision decisions?

In addition, when Adele and Zoe shared their revision plans with their classmates, their teachers encouraged those who felt that this method would work for them to try it out. Before the teachers knew it, a whole slew of first and second graders were making similar re-vision plans—each one perfectly tailored to the student's particular needs. Imagine how empowering this must have been for Adele and Zoe—and for their classmates!

Teaching our writers how to develop their own tools is infinitely more sustainable than using preexisting tools. Quick survey: How many of you use the graphic organizer your sixth-grade teacher taught you to use to write a persuasive piece? That graphic organizer may have been helpful to you then (although I doubt it was helpful to 100 percent of your classmates), but how useful is it to you now? Having spent much of your adult life reading a wide variety of blog posts, letters to the editor, and *New York Times* opinion pieces, as well as viewing political ads and documentaries like *Blackfish* and *Where to Invade Next*, you have likely come to the conclusion that most graphic organizers we offer students for the purpose of persuading an audience are almost laughably inadequate. (In the spirit of camaraderie, I have included one in Figure 4.5 that I developed for my middle school stu-dents sometime during my first ten years of teaching.) If not inadequate, such tools nonetheless lead to the kind of stilted writing that would never in a million years make its way into a community newsletter, much less the *New York Times*.

As an example, let's look at a preexisting tool one group of teachers created to help their third-grade students write a short descriptive piece about a special or favorite place: the ubiquitous web. In the center of the web, students are directed to identify their special or favorite place. The tool asks students to "add details about your topic in the circles provid-ed," saving their *sensory* details for the square at the bottom right. One student, Isaiah, has chosen to write about his favorite frozen-yogurt haunt. You can see by looking at his web (Figure 4.6) that he has done precisely what the tool has directed him to do. How effective was this tool at helping ten-year-old Isaiah write the descriptive piece in Figure 4.7? (I'll wait while you read; take your time.)

Name: _____   Block: _____

Sub Sandwich Graphic Organizer

Introduction (TOP BUN) — Include Position Being Argued!

Argument #1 (CHEESE) + Evidence & Examples (MAYO)

Argument #2 (HAM) + Evidence & Examples (MUSTARD)

Argument #3 (SALAMI) + Evidence & Examples (PICKLES)

Conclusion (BOTTOM BUN)

FIGURE 4.5
Sub Sandwich Graphic Organizer

Name: _____   **My Special Place/My Favorite Place**

Writing Prompt: Write a descriptive paragraph about a place that is your favorite to go to or special to you in some way. Tell why this place is special to you or why it is your favorite place to visit. Help people use their senses to 'visit' your place in their mind, even if they have not ever visited there.

Organization Web: Fill in the center of the web with your special or favorite place. Then add details about your topic in the circles provided. Fill in one detail for each of the senses listed in the square.

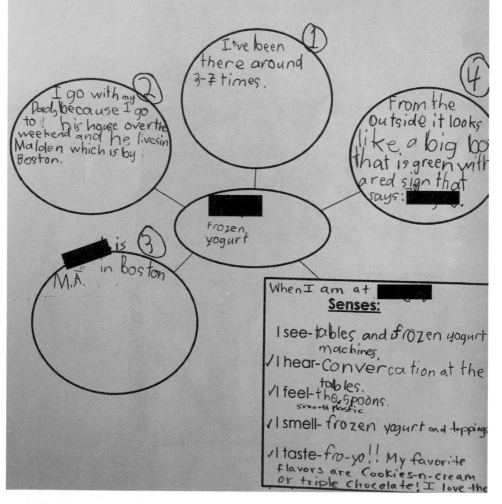

I've been there around 3-7 times. ①

I go with my Dad, because I go to his house over the weekend and he lives in Malden which is by Boston. ②

From the Outside it looks like a big bo that is green with a red sign that says: ④

frozen yogurt

is ③
M.A. in Boston

When I am at ____
Senses:

I see- tables and frozen yogurt machines.
✓ I hear- Convercation at the tables.
✓ I feel- the spoons.
   smooth plastic
✓ I smell- frozen yogurt and toppings
✓ I taste- fro-yo!! My favorite flavors are Cookies-n-cream or triple chocolate! I love the

FIGURE 4.6
Isaiah's web

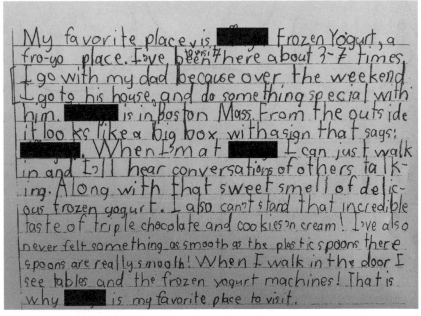

FIGURE 4.7
Isaiah's final piece

The point here is *not* to disparage Isaiah's brave attempt at writing this piece, nor is it to malign the hard work of his teachers. (We've all been there; recall Figure 4.5.) Let's be frank with one another, though: how effectively does Isaiah describe his favorite place? Does his description make you want to go there? Do the details make sense, or do they seem like they were just plopped in there, one after the other? When I first read this piece, I felt as if the heart of it—what I, as a reader, wanted to know more about—was the fact the frozen-yogurt bar is where Isaiah and his dad go when they want to "do something special" with one another. But the tool that Isaiah was asked to use in order to "organize" his composition before drafting it does not support providing more information about this important detail; instead, it hangs there, isolated from the other details. And although Isaiah includes several interesting descriptions—the "smooth" plastic spoons, the way the building looks like a "big box" from the outside—one

FIGURE 4.8
A blank writing journal

has to wonder how Isaiah would've described the place had he used a different kind of tool—especially one that *he himself created.*

To offer another example of how preexisting tools can limit writers, let's take a brief but close look at primary writing journals (like the one shown in Figure 4.8).

Although these journals can certainly provide an organizational "scaffold" for students, freeing them up to focus on the content of their writing, they are not without their problems. For one, the way the pages are organized makes it difficult for our youngest writers to make meaningful decisions about how to lay out their text or illustrations, an important craft element. In today's world of dynamic and complex picture books, arguably the most familiar kind of book to students in kindergarten through second grade, it is very difficult to find one that organizes each page the same way, with the illustration *always* located on the top half of the page and the text *always* on the bottom half of the page. For another, these journals provide little to no opportunity or space for students to add such elements as a cover, a title page, a dedication, or a series of end pages to their compositions. Although not every student chooses to compose a picture book during writing workshop, if the only option she has is to write in a primary writing journal—a tool used in a large number of primary classrooms—we can almost *guarantee* that she won't. And that would be a darn shame.

Renewing Our Use of "Tools" in the Writing Workshop

Setting aside the fact that my husband and I are *still* struggling to convince our daughters to help out more often at home, I can acknowledge that we have managed to make some progress (however small; parenting is hard!). For one, we have learned to include our daughters in the broader conversation about chores, which has helped us empower *them* to make decisions about who should be responsible for what and when. (Example: our oldest daughter is a competitive gymnast who attends ten hours of practice a week, and thus is only responsible for chores on her nonpractice days.) For another, we have each shared what kinds of reminders (or "tools") work for us personally: my oldest and her father prefer to use digital reminders, while my youngest and I like to use sticky notes or good old-fashioned paper and tape to keep ourselves in line. Perhaps most importantly, instead of asking the girls specifically to "do the dishes" or "take out the trash," David and I have taught them to be more aware of their surroundings and to make intentional decisions about what chores need to be done. (No more spoons in the drawer? Perhaps the dishwasher needs to be unloaded.)

Our method isn't perfect, nor are our tools. (We still occasionally find ourselves tripping over piles of dirty socks that mysteriously multiply overnight.) But changing our tools and the ways in which we use them have helped our daughters become much more thoughtful and independent members of the household than they would be otherwise. Likewise, making a concerted effort to change the tools we use to help our student writers—and the ways in which we use them in our classrooms (see Table 4.2 for ideas)—is bound to develop more thoughtful, independent writers who have agency, who make intentional decisions about their work, and who will have developed effective strategies ("tools") that meet their specific needs and that are likely to last far beyond any particular lesson, unit, or school year. What could be more meaningful than that?

TABLE 4.2

Premade Tool Tune-Up 101

INSTEAD OF USING . . .*	CONSIDER . . .	QUESTIONS YOU MIGHT ASK STUDENTS TO HELP SUPPORT THIS WORK
Graphic organizers	*Reading a wide variety of mentors and collaboratively discussing/charting common features, traits, craft moves; asking student mentors to share their planning/organizing/drafting processes*	What do you notice about the way this text was written? How might we map it out? How might we use what we know about our favorite texts to help us plan or map out our own work?
Revising checklists	*Teaching students to be mindful, critical readers of one another's work; facilitating a whole-class or small-group inquiry into word choice, punctuation, sentence structure, etc.*	How does the author use punctuation to help us know how to read his or her writing? How can we respond to one another's work as readers in order to make it better?
Story starters or writing prompts	*Mining interviews with authors and illustrators and charting/documenting the many ways that they generate ideas*	How did you get your ideas for writing today? How does the author get his or her ideas? Would that work for you?
Preformatted writing paper (e.g., lined paper) or digital templates	*Collaboratively identifying ways that students might format paper to match their particular needs; facilitating an inquiry into layout decisions that authors and illustrators make in their work*	What do you need to help you write/illustrate here? How might these different formats affect how you compose this piece? How might they affect how your readers receive this piece?
"Words to use instead of" displays	*Facilitating a targeted word study inquiry or documenting and sharing lists of words from students' independent reading or class read-alouds*	When does it make sense to change up the words we use? How does our word choice affect how our writing is received by our readers?
Writing process displays	See Chapter 2: Renew How We Teach Writing Process	
Writing rubrics	See Chapter 5: Renew How We Assess & Evaluate Student Writing	

*EXTREMELY IMPORTANT NOTE THAT I WISH I COULD PUT IN 72-POINT FONT: Please know that I am not advocating for *never* using tools like these. That would be ridiculous. Rather, I am advocating for a more balanced approach to how we use tools in our classrooms.

*All writers assess writing as we go, hesitating slightly as
we make judgements about what word works best or what
ideas should come next. Every writing choice we make
springs from some assessment that we've already made.*

—Maja Wilson

. . . .

CHAPTER 5

Renew How We Assess & Evaluate Student Writing

I t's not easy being the parent of a competitive gymnast. Even recreational ones, like my oldest daughter Gianna, spend enough
practice hours at the gym that it becomes like a second home—
an ugly, box-shaped, stinky home that I could probably drive to in my
sleep (all I'd have to do is follow the odor, after all). As a "gym parent,"
I must always have enough food in the house to sustain my daughter's
need for two nutrient-packed dinners: one for her to scarf down before
practice, and one for her to inhale *after* practice as she's heading to
bed. Plus, as much as my husband and I enjoy watching her compete,
it's slightly annoying to sacrifice five to six hours of every weekend
during competition season for a measly three- or four-minute window
of watching her *actually* compete.

If all this weren't enough, it can be challenging to offer the appropriate response to Gianna's performance after each competition. As a member of a recreational team, Gianna's main goal is to work hard and do her best on each event (floor, beam, bars, and vault), but all in the name of fun—this isn't the Junior Olympics, after all. But occasionally, she will leave a meet majorly bummed out about a score she received that she didn't think matched her performance. What can we say to that? It all looks amazing to us, sitting there on the sidelines. (We sure as heck could never do what she and her teammates do, even at our most fit.) Plus, the judges she has for one competition often change from meet to meet and from event to event. So what looks like a 8.95 vault to one judge one week might score a 9.05 at the next meet, despite being nearly identical. The vast majority of meet judges at least *try* to be objective in their scoring, which is itself incredibly complicated. (One scoring guidebook I found online runs over sixty pages!) But meet judges, like writing teachers, are human. And although gymnasts are judged on what can sometimes amount to a ten-second event, I see a lot of similarities in the way gymnasts and writers are assessed and evaluated by others.

Rethinking How We Assess & Evaluate Student Writers

Just as a gymnast is so much more than his or her score on an individual event (memories of Mckayla Maroney's final vault at the 2012 Summer Olympics come to mind), a student writer is so much more than his or her score on a given piece of writing. We *know* this as teachers; there isn't one of us who would deny it. Yet many of us continue to be satisfied by the practice of declaring an overall score. Even when using rubrics to assess and evaluate students' compositions that include multiple sets of criteria (for organization, voice, conventions, etc.), we are often comfortable averaging the scores that students receive on each area so we can write "B–" or "3.7" on a piece of work. (See Box 5.1 for information on the differences between *assessment* and *evaluation*.)

What message or "story" are we sending our student writers with a single overall score? Not only does it imply that their worth as a writer can be whittled down to one letter or number (which itself can mean different things for different teachers and even within different units of study), but that the worth of *writing itself* can be whittled down this way. In her book *Rethinking Rubrics in Writing Assessment* (2006), Maja Wilson demonstrates the absurdity of this practice by comparing it with the kinds of conversations we have about literature—about what *real writers write*—both in and out of school:

> *Imagine how quickly the conversation in a book club would be cut short if our meetings revolved around representing our responses to the latest best-seller in numbers:* Poisonwood Bible-*voice, 5; organization, 3. We might introduce these rankings as an inside English teacher joke, but the numbers would never be the focus of our time together. (29)*

Those of us who work in states whose public schools are annually given a single comprehensive grade (Maine, for example) understand how frustrating it can be to receive a grade that is not reflective of the blood, sweat, and tears that we've poured into our work. (This is admittedly not a perfect analogy, as many of the factors that feed into a school grading system like Maine's are completely out of the control of its educators.) How would Barbara Kingsolver react to us giving her best-selling novel a 4, thrown in with a handful of notes scribbled in the margins? Moreover, how would she—or any other author—react to being given an overall letter grade for the body of work she produced in a given span of time?

A single overall score also sends the message that a reader's response to writing can be made objective if we just try hard enough.

But *is this even possible?* Moreover, is it desirable? Louise Rosenblatt, a pioneering educational researcher whose work has had an enormous influence on the teaching of literature, frequently wrote of her widely lauded "transactional theory" of reading, whereby the reader and the text interact to create meaning. In her 1956 essay "The Acid Test for Literature Teaching," she writes, "when we teach literature, we are . . . concerned with the particular and personal way in which students learn to infuse meaning into the pattern of printed symbols" (1956, 67). I would flip this notion on its head to suggest that when we *read* literature (i.e., students' compositions), we should not be afraid of the *particular* and *personal* way in which we, as readers, respond to students' "printed symbols"—that we embrace the subjectivity inherent in responding to writing, are transparent about it, and use it as a way to teach our student writers about the value of a reader's (or an audience's) response to writing.

BOX 5.1: Assessment vs. Evaluation

Although the terms *assessment* and *evaluation* are sometimes used interchangeably, it's worth noting how they're different. The term *assessment* derives from the Latin *assidere,* which means "sit beside." It is, or should be, interactive: done *with* students, not *to* them. When we talk about *assessing* students, it is for the purpose of identifying the following elements, among others:

- What students *know* or *can do* (or can demonstrate or articulate* that they know or can do);
- What students have *learned* over a period of time (or how effectively we have *taught* them what we want them to know or be able to do);
- What our next instruction might look like (or how we might help students progress in their learning).

Alternatively, when we talk about *evaluating* students, it is for the purpose of articulating to others (students, families, administration) what *we think* students know or can do and of judging, sorting, and categorizing them.

Although it would be impossible to *evaluate* a student's learning without first *assessing* it, in theory, it is possible—and, I would argue, desirable—to *assess* learning without *evaluating* it.

*The ability of a student to *demonstrate* or *articulate* his or her learning can often be mistaken for *the learning itself;* however, anyone who has ever had difficulty performing on a test or talking about his or her learning in front of another individual knows that these are actually two very separate entities.

Revising How We Assess & Evaluate Student Writers

I'd love to say that no educator would ever *think* of reducing a kindergarten or first-grade student's composition to a single overall score, but that would be a lie. I have had numerous friends and family members send me photographic evidence of this very practice occurring. (And each time this happens, I'll be honest: a small piece of my soul shrivels up and dies.) Happily, I've seen many *more* examples of assessments communicated through narrative comments—or better yet, considering the limited reading ability of our youngest students, through the practice of regular conferring.

In Becky Wright's kindergarten class, students' compositional skills are assessed from the very first day, when they are invited to "make books" during writing workshop. As Becky moves about the room, conferring with students one-on-one or in small groups, she takes notes about what she is noticing that they can do (e.g., "Daryl is writing letterlike symbols on the cover of his book," "Emerson is using color to differentiate between her characters") or—more often, because sometimes it's just too difficult to take useful notes when conferring with a roomful five-year-olds—takes photos of their work with her smartphone to reflect on later. Sometimes, Becky will use a conferring tool that works for *her*—like the modified version of one Katie Wood Ray and Matt Glover developed and introduced in their 2011 book *Watch Katie and Matt ... Sit Down and Teach Up* (see Figure 5.1)—to help focus her assessment on specific areas or concepts.

No matter what tools Becky uses to document her assessment of student work, she is careful to communicate her thinking with students as she engages them in conversation about her "noticings," asks them questions about the compositional decisions they've made, and nudges them to take "healthy risks" by trying a new skill or idea they discussed during the day's mini-lesson. In addition, she regularly engages her students in reflecting on their own work, their individual processes, and their evolving writing identities.

For Becky and her students, *this is enough.* There is no need to go any further—not until the end of the trimester, anyway, which I address later—by holistically evaluating students' compositions using a letter grade, a numerical score, a marked-up rubric, or a "Good Job!" sticker.

If this kind of assessment is good enough for our youngest writers, why can't it be good enough for writers of all ages? As the "lead learner" in the room (for most of the time, anyway), we teachers have a responsibility to regularly assess our students' work, engage them in conversation about their compositional decisions, offer them feedback that will help them grow as writers, and help them reflect on their own experiences as writers. We can do this most effectively through our conferring, just as Becky does with her students. (See Box 5.2 for the conferring resources that have been most helpful in my own development as a conferrer.)

ESSENTIAL UNDERSTANDINGS ABOUT TEXTS

Is the writing *about* something?	Is there an organization to the writing? A connection between ideas?	When the student reads the writing, does it *sound* like a piece of writing?	Is the student writing *in the manner* of other writing s/he's seen or heard?	Does the content/org. of the piece reflect what you want the student to understand about this genre and/or modality?	Is the content of the writing effectively communicated (spelling, grammar, mechanics)?

ESSENTIAL UNDERSTANDINGS ABOUT PROCESS

Is the student intentional about what s/he is representing on the page?	Does s/he engage in revision while composing?	Is there any evidence s/he is thinking ahead about what s/he'll write next?	Has s/he made any intentional crafting decisions in the composition?	How long has the student worked on this composition? In one sitting? Over time?	Does s/he exhibit a willingness to solve problems as s/he writes?

ESSENTIAL UNDERSTANDINGS ABOUT WHAT IT MEANS TO BE A WRITER

How (and why) has the student decided to write this particular piece?	How interested is the student in an audience's or reader's response to this book?	Has the student composed in a way that led him to new meaning as he was writing?	Can I see in this piece that the student has been willing to take compositional risks?	Does it seem as if this student has a sense of self as a writer? A sense of history, strengths, voice, etc.?	Does she show she understands her powerful position as author of this piece?

Additional notes:

FIGURE 5.1

Becky uses this conferring sheet to take notes. (Adapted from Ray and Glover [2011].)

BOX 5.2: Three Conferring Resources That Have
Transformed My Practice

Let's face it: conferring effectively is *difficult*. As with learning to parent
or become a competitive gymnast, there is no distinct "end game";
learning to confer well is a lifelong process. Though there are many
conferring books and videos on the market for educators to peruse,
these three have been invaluable to my own professional practice.

Watch Katie and Matt... Sit Down and Teach Up by Katie Wood Ray and
Matt Glover (2011)

This is one of those professional texts that has so affected my teaching
that I am astonished it hasn't "blown up" the way some others have.
While most of the videos featured in this multimedia book are geared
toward pre-K through second grade, the lessons that Katie and Matt
share about their own development as educators extend above and
beyond any particular grade level.

How's It Going? A Practical Guide to Conferring with Writers by Carl
Anderson (2000)

A classic go-to book among educators interested in increasing
the effectiveness of their conferring, *How's It Going?* is chock-full
of practical advice, helpful strategies, and sample transcripts of
Anderson's own conversations with students.

Let's Talk: Managing One-on-One, Peer, and Small-Group Conferences by
Mark Overmeyer (2015)

Because one-on-one conferring should not be the only tool in our
assessment toolbox, Mark shows us how "talk" in a variety of settings
(small group, whole class, peer-to-peer, etc.) can help lift the level
of writing and engagement among students within a typical writing
workshop.

A Note (or Two) About Peer Conferring and Authentic Audiences

In an ideal world, a teacher would not be the sole reader of a student's compositional work. Spending a significant amount of the school year teaching students to be critical yet compassionate readers and responders to text is a practice that will pay dividends in our student writers' lives. Returning to Louise Rosenblatt and her transactional theory of reading has enormous value here. Although we can—and should—spend significant time talking with students of all ages about what makes an effective informational text, an engaging comic, a heart-wrenching poem, and so on, we should also be transparent about the very particular interests and tastes each reader has that can deem a piece of writing "good" or not. Rubrics, scoring guides, and objective criteria aside, readers of writing are human, and one person's response to a composition may not perfectly align with another's. (If it did, what a drab, boring world we'd be living in!)

One solution to this issue is to offer students a variety of platforms where they might share their writing with authentic audiences (see Box 5.3 for some examples) while at the same time exploring, as a class of readers, the elements that make responses to writing helpful.

BOX 5.3: Some Ideas for Helping Students Write for an Authentic Audience
- Use a safe blogging platform such as Kidblog, Edublogs, or Weebly where students can share anything from essays to comics to poetry with a secure audience (e.g., their families, other classrooms).
- Start a class Instagram, Twitter, or Snapchat account and encourage students to take turns sharing news, photos, and stories about that day's learning.

- Tap into students' strong opinions by having them post reviews—and comment on others'—of restaurants (Yelp), toys or gadgets (Amazon), or books (Goodreads).
- Utilize opportunities for students to engage in authentic discussions across the globe through such sites as Voices of Youth or the *New York Times'* "Student Opinion" feature.
- Write picture books for younger siblings or students and host a series of "PJ" story times where students can read their books to a real-live audience.
- Consider grounding some of your students' compositional work in a problem-based inquiry by offering possible solutions to real-life stakeholders.
- Encourage the use of a host of *intrapersonal* purposes for writing through the regular use of writer's notebooks—e.g., writing to discover, writing to think through a concept or idea, writing as "play"—as a writer's first, most authentic audience is him- or herself.

For example, your class might partner with another class of writers—within your own school or, through the magic of the Internet, with a class halfway across the globe—to read one another's work and examine the kinds of responses that are most useful. Or you can start small and engage in a "mini-inquiry" about feedback within your own classroom using a variety of online resources (see Box 5.4). If our own experiences with peer response are any indication, "I liked it" simply doesn't cut it for most writers. However, the opposite is true as well: when commenters on my blog, for example, deride a post without offering any advice about how to improve it (or the ideas and concepts within), they might as well have skipped commenting altogether for all the help it does me.

Useful peer response can be taught to students of all ages and abilities, as Emily Spear's and Sheryl Horton's students can attest. Within an inquiry their multiage first- and second-grade students embarked on about the kinds of layout decisions authors and illustrators make, Emily and Sheryl embedded a significant amount of instruction in critical peer feedback. They modeled feedback for the whole class, brainstormed with students how to use questioning techniques to help writers reflect on their compositions (e.g., "What kinds of layout decisions did you make in this piece?" "How did you grab the attention of your reader?"), capitalized on brave volunteers who were willing to gather feedback from their peers in a whole-group setting, and regularly turned to published authors and illustrators to learn how feedback helped them revise their own compositions.

Investing in this complex, yet important, work with students helped Emily and Sheryl deepen and extend the assessment of *all* of their students' writing and positioned their students as authentic, critical readers of one another's work.

BOX 5.4: Online Resources for Teaching Peer Critique/Response

- Austin's Butterfly: Building Excellence in Student Work (https://vimeo.com/38247060)
- Critique and Feedback: Management in the Active Classroom (https://vimeo.com/142642998)
- Picture Book Author Melissa Stewart's Revision Timeline (http://www.melissa-stewart.com/timeline/10yr_timeline.html)
- Critical Friends: Collaborating as Writers (Teaching Channel) (https://www.teachingchannel.org/videos/student-writing-peer-review-nea)

Renewing Our Assessment Practice (While Subverting Evaluation & Reporting Mandates)

Just as a judge must ultimately give a score for a gymnast's performance on a specific event, most educators are obligated to report out—both to the students and to others—their evaluation of students' compositional performance over a period of time. This approach makes perfect sense at an athletic competition, where the athletes have *chosen* to be judged or evaluated. I would argue that it *doesn't* make sense in schools, where our primary purpose as educators is not to judge, sort, or categorize students, but to *help them learn*. Which is more likely to help students learn: offering them specific feedback about their work, behavior, or performance, or slapping a score on a piece of paper?

As it turns out, I am not the Empress of the World, so I will (grudgingly) ground my argument in realism. As both "coaches" *and* "judges," nearly every classroom teacher has the dual burden of providing feedback that will help students grow as writers as well as giving them a holistic score that ties all of their learning over a given period of time into one neat (?) little bow. How to make such a judgment—one that is ultimately *sub*jective, despite years of misguided attempts to try to make it *ob*jective—without undermining our careful attempts to help our writers grow though gentle, yet useful, feedback? ("Hey kid, your voice really shines here through your use of parenthetical asides! . . . C+.") Perhaps we might (literally) take a page from Linda Rief's book *Read Write Teach: Choice and Challenge in the Reading-Writing Workshop* (2014). In her eighth-grade class at Oyster River Middle School in Durham, New Hampshire, Linda uses her conferring time to communicate most of her feedback and later, when it's time to evaluate their writing, asks her students to determine their own grades in three separate categories: process, content, and conventions. She then averages *her* grades for each category (which are inevitably higher than those the students give themselves) along with them.

While interning in a sixth-grade classroom at Shapleigh Middle School in Kittery, Maine, nearly two decades ago, my cooperating teachers and I engaged in a similar process. For each writing standard or "benchmark" we were required to assess, evaluate, and report out on, we collaborated with the student on a single numerical score that indicated whether that student "exceeded," "met," "partially met," or "did not meet" the standard. This was the score that was ultimately recorded on that student's report card. Most of the time, as in Linda's experience, the students evaluated themselves much more harshly than we ever did; on those rare occasions when the opposite occurred, we let the students' grades stand—because, really, what difference did it make in their development as writers? None. It's the *assessment*, not the *evaluation*, that informs our instruction of students—and that in turn, informs their learning.

Jess Lifshitz, a fifth-grade teacher near Chicago, has gone even further than offering students a say in their own writing evaluation. In a blog post she wrote, "Writing as Celebration," Jess explains how she invites her student writers to be active partners in their own assessment and evaluation by reserving any critical feedback for the time when students are actively engaged in the *process* of writing and devoting the final part of the process—the evaluation part—to reflecting on and celebrating all the ways that they have grown as writers over the course of a particular unit. In framing evaluation in this way, she writes,

> *Every single one of them [sees] evidence of what they [have] learned to do as a writer. Every single one of them [sees] evidence that . . . what I wanted to focus on [as their teacher] was what they [have] done well. What they [have] learned to do. How they [have] grown as writers. And that. That is a true celebration. (2017)*

FIGURE 5.2

U.S. Navy Rear Admiral (and firecracker) Grace Hopper

The benefits of involving students in regular reflection—never mind in regular *celebration*—of their work are clear. As James H. McMillan and Jessica Hearn write in their 2008 article "Student Self-Assessment: The Key to Stronger Student Motivation and Higher Achievement," "evaluating what [students have] learned, what they still need to work on, and how they can get there can all support deeper understanding rather than superficial knowledge" (46). In "The Reliability, Validity, and Utility of Self-Assessment" (2006), researcher and education professor John A. Ross points out that "differences between self- and teacher assessment can lead to productive teacher-student conversations about student learning needs" and that such work can enhance student motivation, confidence, and achievement. My own experience, as well as the experiences of colleagues who regularly invite their students to self-assess their work, supports this.

I am confident in my belief that few administrators would seriously object to having students collaborate on their grades—if not on their *overall* grade for a course or a semester, then for several major assignments that contribute toward that grade. In the worst-case scenario, however, the best I can offer is the old adage that I have always lived by as an educator, first coined by U.S. Navy Rear Admiral Grace Hopper (a firecracker if there ever was one): "It's easier to ask forgiveness than it is to get permission" (1986; see Figure 5.2). If educators can demonstrate the powerful learning that occurs—and the more positive "stories" about writing that begin to evolve—when we rethink, revise, and renew how we assess and evaluate student composition (and I wholeheartedly believe that we *can*), then it doesn't take a giant cognitive leap to suspect that "forgiveness" will be the very last thing on *anyone's* mind.

We maintain our fictions by not writing ourselves.

—Donald Graves

CHAPTER 6

Renew Our Role as Teachers of Writers

As a student, I was "good" at writing. I learned early on how to look, listen, and read carefully in order to perform—that is, to write—the way my teachers wanted me to. Mr. Carson (recall Chapter 1) and his colleagues would show my classmates and me student samples of "A-quality" papers, and I would internalize their structure, their voice, and their generic content. I would then sit at home in front of my Brother electric typewriter, our local classic rock station playing in the background, and churn out a very similar-sounding piece of writing, almost always resulting in an A and a hastily scrawled *Excellent* at the top of the page.

When I moved on to college, this routine became considerably more challenging, but not impossible. With the exception of two or three writing assignments throughout my entire undergraduate career (most of them from my fiction writing class—*clearly* not my forte), I was still able to maintain the illusory identity of a writer. I use the word *illusory* because even when my favorite professor at the University

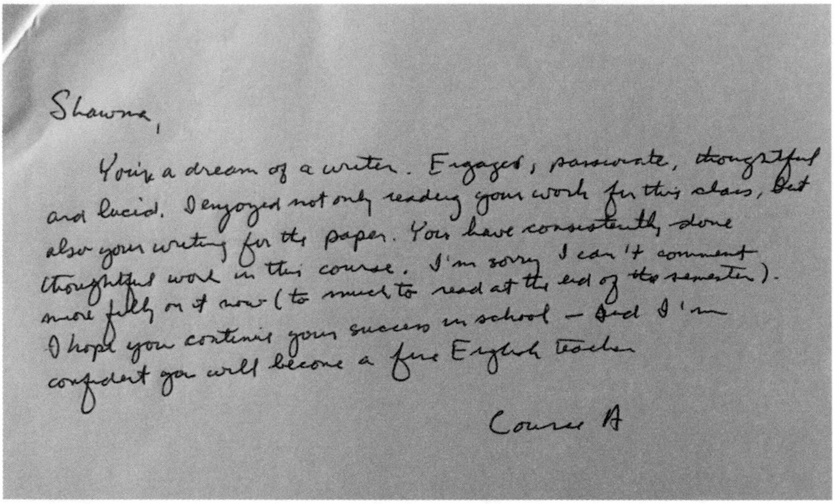

FIGURE 6.1
Yes, I'm bragging here.

of New Hampshire, Tom Newkirk, called me a "dream" of a writer (see Figure 6.1), I still felt like a bit of a fraud—like someone who was merely co-opting the voice, the cadence, and the style of mentors like Dave Barry, Erma Bombeck, and Stephen King (his nonfiction-writing self, not his fiction-writing self). What I didn't understand then was that *this is what writers do*: we "try on" aspects of our favorite mentors' writing identities as we work to develop our own. This is acceptable, normal—even desirable.

Unfortunately, my epiphany didn't materialize until well after I began teaching middle school writers how to write. Let's be honest: that and about *six dozen other epiphanies* I've since experienced about writing didn't materialize until well after I began teaching others to write. Why, you ask?

The answer is simple: because I didn't *actually* write.

I mean, I *wrote*. Throughout a huge chunk of my life I wrote lesson plans, papers for graduate school, long lists for babysitters of what my children would and would not eat. (So obnoxious, right?) I wrote lengthy e-mails, boring meeting notes, and occasional love letters to my husband. I even wrote alongside my students during our regular "freewriting" session at the start of each class and, at least partially, wrote each piece I assigned them. But for most of my life, and certainly for most of those first years as a teacher, I didn't write anything *for myself*. I dabbled in journal writing here and there, and once wrote an essay about being bullied at school that somehow found its way into the pages of the now-defunct *Sassy* magazine (see Figure 6.2), but those moments of writing were few and far between.

So in reality, in at least one glaring aspect—I *was* a fraud.

Because I didn't really write outside of my classroom during those first few years as an educator, my role was relegated to "writer by proxy"—someone who was authorized by the state of New Hampshire

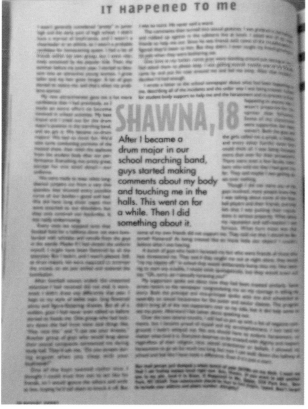

FIGURE 6.2
Brag #2: *Sassy* magazine, August 1993

to "teach" writing, to act on behalf of writers. I read a bazillion books on teaching writing, I used what I had learned through my own experience as a student writer, and, through it all, I honestly and truly believed that I was doing my very best to "teach" students to write. But what I realize now is that the majority of students who left my classroom after those first few years able to "write" left it able to write mostly *school-type* compositions. Only a handful likely went on to write anything of personal substance outside of school, and if they did, it was in spite of, not because of, the role I played as their teacher. (See Box 6.1 for more of my writing epiphanies.)

BOX 6.1: (Very, Very Abbreviated) List of Epiphanies I've Had Since Nurturing a Writing Life Outside of the Classroom

- Despite what many of us are taught as students, genres of writing are not fixed entities. Rather, they ebb and flow based upon social and cultural conventions as well as situational factors.
- Five-paragraph essays do not actually exist in the wild.
- Nor do "character sketches."
- Narrative, persuasive, analytical, and expository types of writing are not mutually exclusive from one another.
- When we write, although there are many times when we choose the genre or form of our composition first, there are also times when genre or form chooses *us*—in other words, *how* we wish to express an idea or inform others may not become clear until we are well into our compositional process.
- Surprise! Writing is not (necessarily) a linear process—nor do all writers employ the same process. (See Chapter 2 for more on this.)
- Eating blackberry scones can significantly enhance writing production.

- Approximately 99.765 percent of what we compose will never make it anywhere beyond our notebooks. That's okay. What we *do* compose, even partially, inside our notebooks is equally as valuable as what we compose and share outside of our notebooks.
- For some writers, talk is an essential part of the composing process. And I don't *only* mean "on task" talking; believe me when I say that if I didn't have my friend Kathy Collins to chat with about local gossip or the latest Kanye-Swift feud when we were both supposed to be "writing," this book may never have made it into your hands. And that would be a darn shame.

Rethinking Our Role as Teachers of Writers

In *Writing: Children & Teachers at Work* (2003), Donald Graves assures us that, thankfully, "teachers don't have to be expert writers to 'write' with the children" (43). He does maintain, however, that writing with our students as a form of "modeling" allows us to more effectively develop community, helps us understand what we see and hear when we observe our students write, and provides multiple opportunities to shed light on the "mysterious" world of writing. Although this is all true, I would argue that doing this *isn't enough*. When we *only* write alongside our students, or between the hours of 7:00 AM and 3:00 PM, we are telling a very limited (and limit*ing*) story about composition—one that often, but not always, fails to take into account, among other things,

- how different spaces and places influence our writing, particularly our output;
- authentic uses (and misuses) of time in writer's lives; and

- the enormous amount of composing writers do "in our heads," long before we produce anything on paper or screen.

In addition, when we (at least semi-regularly) engage in a habit of writing outside of the type we model in class, we become much more empathetic toward the myriad struggles that writers experience on a very regular basis—struggles like trying to draft a measly 600 words without obsessively checking your social media feed every sixty (okay, thirty) seconds. Or like spending hours searching for that *just right* word or phrase and, for some psychotic reason, not granting yourself permission to move on until you find it. Or overcoming the urge to catch up on episodes of *The Bachelor* while scarfing down a bowl of Doritos rather than compose *anything*.

Even more importantly, when we engage in a semi-regular habit of writing, we can much more genuinely speak to those incredibly fantastic moments that writers experience on occasion, like the amazing feeling of completing a particularly difficult draft or writing something that makes a reader spontaneously laugh out loud. Anyone who's ever taught a group of students of any age knows that when we are faking our way through something, or at the very least "phoning it in" by *only* engaging on a superficial level with what we are purporting to teach, students can smell our lack of authenticity a mile away. They know, even subconsciously, that they are being sold a decidedly moldy bill of goods.

Revising Our Role as Teachers of Writers

I sense that some of you might be reading this with a bit of a scowl on your face. Your eyes have narrowed and your shoulders have started to droop. Perhaps you've let out more than one deep sigh within the past several minutes. You might be thinking, "How can I *possibly* make time to write for myself with everything else I have to do?" You're imagining how cumbersome it would be to attempt to hold a pen and notebook while in warrior pose.

Don't despair! Just as Donald Graves reminds us that you don't have to be an expert writer to write with children, I am here to assure you that you don't have to blog, write for *Education Week,* or publish a book of poems to be a "writer." In her book *What You Know by Heart: How to Develop Curriculum for Your Writing Workshop* (2002), Katie Wood Ray kindly reminds us that "as teachers of writing, we don't need to write a lot or even very often" (5). Not all writers live by the maxim made famous by Donald Murray, *nulla dies sine linea* ("never a day without a line")—nor should they. They all must cultivate their own individual habits and processes for writing. But if we truly value the deep understandings we develop when we nurture ourselves as writers—understandings that we can then help our students come to develop in our revised role as teacher—then we must make time to write outside of our classrooms.

The good news is that there are many ways to nurture a semi-regular habit of writing, especially if we broaden our ideas about what writing "is" (as I argued we do in Chapter 3) (see Box 6.2). However, as with all habits, we must put in the time and effort to make them so. Anyone who's ever developed and then swiftly broken a New Year's resolution related to increasing their personal fitness level knows this to be true. The truth is, we don't acquire a new habit if it is anything less than engaging—by which I don't *necessarily* mean 100 percent fun, but rather (at least somewhat) stimulating, entertaining, or captivating. Just as we must work intentionally to make writing engaging for our students, so must we do the same for ourselves.

BOX 6.2: Six Ideas for Nurturing a Semi-Regular Writing Habit

1. Sit down with a cup of tea (or a nice cold brew) at one of your favorite local hot spots. Spend some time transcribing the conversation(s) you hear around you. What do you notice? What do you wonder? What possibilities for writing come from this totally acceptable and professionally sanctioned form of eavesdropping? (Shout-out to the handful of folks who have turned me onto this delightful practice!)

2. Write lists. Lists are fast, easy, and can be added to and expanded upon in infinite ways. One of my favorite mentor lists of all time is one I've shared with colleagues repeatedly. It's from Jerry Spinelli's memoir *Knots in My Yo-Yo String* and is called "Thirteen Things I Wished I Could Do." (It's no coincidence that several of my own blog posts have been written in list form, or that two of the four pieces I've written for The Nerdy Book Club have been for their "Top Ten List" posts.) Some of my favorite list-type entries in my writer's notebooks are ones that are actually sketches of things, such as that found in Figure 6.3 ("Things I Wish I Loved, But Don't").

FIGURE 6.3
From my writer's notebook

3. Compose some encyclopedia entries about your life. Don't make that face! I'm serious. If you've read Amy Krouse Rosenthal's *Encyclopedia of an Ordinary Life*, you know that personal encyclopedia entries can be incredibly witty, thoughtful, and inspiring. In addition, they can be varying lengths and can take the form of sketches, paragraphs, lists(!), charts, timelines, and so on. Read a few of Amy's entries and try some of your own, or go rogue and compose some fictional entries about a made-up character's life.

4. Write a bunch of "long sentences." This idea is inspired by Tom Newkirk, who himself was inspired by a piece that he found in Jerome Stern's *Micro Fiction* and that was written as a "single, 250-word sentence" (2009, 31). Tom shares his own draft of a short-story-as-single-sentence (as well as a spectacular one that a former student wrote) on pages 31–33 of his book *Holding On to Good Ideas in a Time of Bad Ones*.

5. Try your hand at a six-word story or memoir. I'm sure you've heard of the famous six-word story that most people attribute to Ernest Hemingway: *For sale: baby shoes, never worn.* While this oft-told legend of the origin of the six-word story has been challenged, the appeal of the form remains real—and it's an accessible enough genre to convince even the most reluctant or novice writer to try. (If you want to challenge yourself further, follow the example of Don Goble, a multimedia teacher, author, and Apple Distinguished Educator, who asks students to turn their six-word stories into a digital/video version that he calls "Six Unique Shots." See more at http://lhstv.weebly.com/6-word-stories—6-shot-videos.html.)

6. Grab a copy of one of the following books and play, play, PLAY. Unleash your inner writer/sketcher/COMPOSER!

   • *Art Before Breakfast: A Zillion Ways to Be More Creative No Matter How Busy You Are* by Danny Gregory (2015)

- *Syllabus: Notes from an Accidental Professor* by Lynda Barry (2014)
- *Steal Like an Artist: 10 Things Nobody Told You About Being Creative* & *Steal Like an Artist Journal* by Austin Kleon (2012)
- *How to Make a Journal of Your Life* by Dan Price (1999)
- *Living Out Loud: Activities to Fuel a Creative Life* by Keri Smith (2003)
- *Scribble It! 30 Postcards* by Taro Gomi (2010)

The tricky part is that what is engaging to one of us might not be engaging to someone else, so I can only offer some advice that has worked for both myself and for those I know personally. One of the ways I have engaged my own colleagues in the act of writing is through monthly sessions I developed that are loosely based on the Teachers Write! Virtual summer writing camp (http://www.katemessner.com/teachers-write/) created by author Kate Messner (see Figure 6.4).

During these sessions, which are entirely optional, we 1) read, view, or listen to something that I hope will provoke a feeling, a thought, or a memory in my colleagues; 2) brainstorm and discuss possibilities for writing, and 3) WRITE. This writing often takes the form of a wide variety of compositions, from stream-of-consciousness prose to poetry to sketches to lists—anything goes! Then, just when it feels as though my colleagues are really diving deep into their compositions, I abruptly stop them. I do this intentionally, as I want them to be interrupted when they are *in medias res*—in the midst of something—so that they will be more compelled to return to it later. We always finish our sessions with two important components:

- a process share, where we talk with one another about what happened when we were writing, what it felt like, where we struggled or stared off into space or doodled in our notebooks; and

- a brief discussion of the implications for our own work with students—what we can learn from our own experience as writers that we can then use to increase the effectiveness of our instruction.

More than once, colleagues have expressed to me that these sessions have done more for them, both personally and professionally, than any other professional learning opportunities I have provided.

If you don't have a colleague who is willing to coordinate a writing group of this kind and lack the confidence, time, or motivation to do so yourself, there are other ways to engage in writing groups that meet regularly; that offer space, time, and opportunities to compose and share with one another; and that support the difficult and challenging work of nurturing a semi-regular habit of writing. The Slice

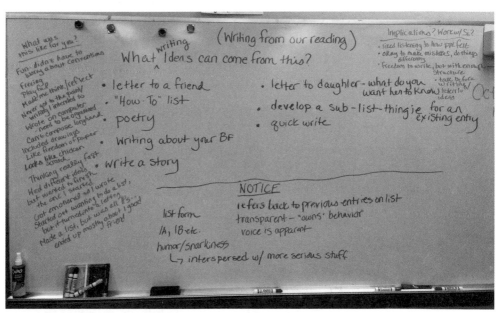

FIGURE 6.4
Notes from one of our Teachers Write! sessions

of Life challenge (https://twowritingteachers.org/challenges/) from the *Two Writing Teachers* blog is one of the most popular among my colleagues on Twitter and offers a month-long challenge that involves starting a blog, composing and posting a brief "Slice of Life" story each day throughout the month, and providing a link to your post via *Two Writing Teachers*. If this sounds too involved or scary, consider taking part in Linda Urban's #WriteDaily30 challenge (see Figures 6.5–6.7), where the only commitment needed is to compose *something* (a sentence, a paragraph, a sketch) once a day for thirty consecutive days, or Debbie Ohi's Daily Words challenge (http://inkygirl.com/dailywords), which you can customize to meet your specific writing needs. Whatever method, platform, or strategy you use to nurture a semi-regular habit of writing is worth it if it works.

There is an elephant in the room (or rather, on the page) that I must acknowledge before we move on. For many of us, writing for ourselves is not a matter of finding the *time* to write, but rather of finding the *courage* to write. Even for someone like me, who has always "identified" as a writer, just the thought of opening myself up to scrutiny—regardless of whether or not I intend to *share* my writing—can be terrifying. Because writing is, essentially, thinking, whether we do it in print, on paper, visually, or digitally, it is akin to walking around without a protective layer of skin.

In a blog post I wrote in 2016 called "On Being Afraid to Write," I listed some of the things I yearn to write about but am afraid to. Think of how our students must feel! We can likely all agree that most of them are also afraid of

- looking or sounding stupid ("I can't write/spell/articulate my ideas/hold a pencil/type"),

- sharing their work ("Everyone will make fun of me/criticize me/reject me"), and

- being misunderstood ("No one will get what I really mean").

FIGURES 6.5, 6.6, 6.7 Participants in the #WriteDaily30 challenge

Hmm. Sound familiar? It sure does to me. As writers, we share many of the same fears. As I wrote in my blog post, "The mere act of writing always, in some small way, affirms some aspect of ourselves, of who we are at our most raw. In short, the act of writing forces us to simultaneously ask and answer the question: *Am I a good person?*" But if we cannot bring *ourselves* to face that fear head-on—to slay the writing beast—how in the world can we ever ask our students to?

Short answer: we can't.

Renewing Our Role as Teachers of Writers

For too long, educators have been maligned by that age-old quote: "Those who can, do. Those who can't do, teach." (The original quote, attributed to George Bernard Shaw in his book *Maxims for Revolutionists*, has been slightly modified over the years, but its sting remains the same.) Engaging in one or more of the acts I described in this chapter in order to nurture a semi-regular habit of writing knocks that ridiculous adage straight onto its bony old tush and benefits our student writers in ways that no amount of professional development in writing instruction ever could.

This cannot (yet) be proven by research; I have no statistics to offer for how being a teacher-writer significantly narrows the so-called "achievement gap." But I hope by now you understand that this sort of data pales in comparison to that which we collect and observe every day in our classrooms. It pales in comparison to the significance of the stories we tell our students about what it means to be a writer. And it pales in comparison to the renewal we will feel once we cast off the burden of maintaining our fictions—our roles as "writers by proxy"—by failing to write ourselves (see Box 6.3).

BOX 6.3: The "Teachers as Writers" Debate

I am not the first, and will certainly not be the last, to argue that teachers of writers should themselves write. One of the most interesting moments in this age-old debate occurred in 1990, when the National Council of Teachers of English periodical *The English Journal* published a piece (ironically) written by high school English teacher Karen Jost called "Rebuttal: Why High-School Writing Teachers Should Not Write." Jost wrote this piece in response to the "dictum" of those in academia, including the University of New Hampshire's own Donald Murray, that "writing teachers should write." In response, the editors of *The English Journal* received a flood of letters supporting Jost (almost five to one, according to their calculations a few months after the piece was first published). Not content to sit silently observing this renewed debate take place, the National Writing Project published a piece by Tim Gillespie, codirector of the Oregon Writing Project, in their September 1991 *Quarterly* called "Joining the Debate: *Shouldn't Writing Teachers Write?*" Jost's piece as well as Gillespie's reflection on the controversy are both well worth reading.

Afterword

At present, my husband, David, and I would consider ourselves to be near-perfect parents. Our household is immaculate; our children rarely squabble; we live and breathe an air of pure bliss almost every moment of every day.

KIDDING! Like all parents, we sometimes—no, oftentimes—struggle. We make mistakes. We second-guess our decisions on behalf of our children.

But we no longer feel as hopeless as we once did; we no longer worry that we're horrible parents. We have internalized a habit of rethinking, revising, and—most important—*renewing* our parenting practices, which has helped us crawl out from the "sinkhole" of helpless complacency. As a result, we are much more responsive to the varied and individual needs of our two children. (NOTE: If one or more of them end up writing a sordid tell-all about our family life somewhere down the line, you have my permission to burn this book.) This work took *years*, and it will take my husband and me quite literally the rest of our lives to continue honing our parenting skills.

As an educator, I know this to be similarly true: for the entirety of my professional life, I will continually be working to improve my practice. But rather than feel disheartened or dismayed by this, I feel exactly the opposite: I feel hopeful. Inspired. And by using a framework to rethink and revise my work based on my current students' needs and the stories they're told through my instructional practices, I am confident that I will continue along this renewable, self-sustaining path, envisioning new possibilities for the work we engage in together.

Like all teachers, I will sometimes—no, oftentimes—struggle. I will make mistakes. I will second-guess the decisions I make on behalf of myself and my students.

There's one thing, however, that I've promised that I will *never* do, and that is to become complacent in my work. Because the truth of the matter is, our students deserve better.

Our profession deserves better.

We deserve better.

References

Ainsworth, Shaaron, Vaughan Prain, and Russell Tytler. 2011. "Drawing to Learn in Science." *Science Magazine.* http://www.hostos.cuny.edu/MTRJ/HTRT/Drawing_Science%202011.pdf.

Alexander, Kwame. 2016. "Questions and Answers with Kwame Alexander." *Kwame Alexander.* http://kwamealexander.com/about/me/c/199/.

Anderson, Carl. 2000. *How's It Going? A Practical Guide to Conferring with Student Writers.* Portsmouth, NH: Heinemann.

Barnett, Mac, and Jon Klassen. 2014. *Sam and Dave Dig a Hole.* Somerville, MA: Candlewick Press.

Barry, Lynda. 2014. *Syllabus: Notes from an Accidental Professor.* Montreal: Drawn & Quarterly.

Bell, Cece. 2014. *El Deafo.* New York: Amulet Books.

———. 2015. "Cece Bell: How I Made El Deafo—in Pictures." *The Guardian.* August 4. http://www.theguardian.com/childrens-books-site/gallery/2015/aug/04/cece-bell-el-deafo-in-pictures.

Coppola, Shawna. 2016. "On Being Afraid to Write." *My So-Called Literacy Life.* https://mysocalledliteracylife.com/2016/04/29/on-being-afraid-to-write/.

Danielson, Julie. 2011a. "Seven Questions Over Breakfast with Jon Klassen." *Seven Impossible Things Before Breakfast.* http://blaine.org/sevenimpossiblethings/?p=2189.

———. 2011b. "Seven Questions Over Breakfast with John Rocco." *Seven Impossible Things Before Breakfast.* http://blaine.org/sevenimpossible-things/?p=2143.

———. 2014. "7-Imp's 7 Kicks #399: Featuring Marla Frazee." *Seven Impossible Things Before Breakfast.* http://blaine.org/sevenimpossible-things/?p=3532.

Dewey, John. 1893. "Self-Realization as the Moral Ideal." *The Philosophical Review* 2 (6): 652.

———. 1910. *How We Think.* Boston: D.C. Heath.

Dewey, John, and Evelyn Dewey. 1915. *Schools of To-morrow.* New York: Dutton.

Eickholdt, Lisa. 2015. *Learning from Classmates: Using Students' Writing as Mentor Texts.* Portsmouth, NH: Heinemann.

Fletcher, Ralph. N.d. "Ralph Fletcher on Mentor Texts." (Audio blog post.) *Choice Literacy.* https://www.choiceliteracy.com/articles-detail-view.php?id=994.

Frazee, Marla. 2010. *The Boss Baby.* San Diego, CA: Beach Lane Books.

———. 2014. *The Farmer and the Clown.* San Diego, CA: Beach Lane Books.

Fuller, R. Buckminster, and Kiyoshi Kuromiya. 1981. *Critical Path.* New York: St. Martin's Press.

Gillespie, Tim. 1991. "Joining the Debate: *Shouldn't* Writing Teachers Write?" *The Quarterly of the National Writing Project & the Center for the Study of Writing and Literacy* 13 (3): 3–6.

Gomi, Taro. 2010. *Scribble It! 30 Postcards.* San Francisco: Chronicle Books.

Graves, Donald H. 2003. *Writing: Teachers & Children at Work.* 20th anniversary ed. Portsmouth, NH: Heinemann.

Gregory, Danny. 2015. *Art Before Breakfast: A Zillion Ways to Be More Creative No Matter How Busy You Are.* San Francisco: Chronicle Books.

Hanser, Gretchen. 2001. "Juggling the Motor, Language, and Cognitive Demands." (Graphic.) http://www.telability.org/handouts/Telability5_20_2008finalPP.pdf.

Hopper, Grace. 1986. Interview by Diane Hamblen. *Chips Ahoy.* (Newsletter.) July.

Horn, Martha, and Mary Ellen Giacobbe. 2007. *Talking, Drawing, Writing: Lessons for Our Youngest Writers.* Portland, ME: Stenhouse.

Jost, Karen. 1990. "Rebuttal: Why High-School Writing Teachers Should Not Write." *The English Journal* 79 (3): 65–66.

Kleon, Austin. 2012. *Steal Like an Artist: 10 Things Nobody Told You About Being Creative* & *Steal Like an Artist Journal.* New York: Workman.

Lifshitz, Jessica. 2017. "Writing Assessment as Celebration." *Crawling Out of the Classroom.* https://crawlingoutoftheclassroom.wordpress.com/2017/01/16/writing-assessment-as-celebration/.

Mackenzie, Noella. 2011. "From Drawing to Writing: What Happens When You Shift Teaching Priorities in the First Six Months of School?" *Australian Journal of Language and Literacy* 34 (3): 322–340. https://www.alea.edu.au/documents/item/1052.

McMillan, James H. and Jessica Hearn. 2008. "Student Self-Assessment: The Key to Stronger Student Motivation and Higher Achievement." *Educational Horizons* 87 (1): 40–49.

Miller, Donalyn. 2015. "Pinterest Isn't Pedagogy." http://www.txla.org/pinterest-isnt-pedagogy.

Murray, Donald. 1995. *The Craft of Revision.* Revised 2nd ed. San Diego, CA: Harcourt Brace Publishing.

———. 2003. *A Writer Teaches Writing.* Revised 2nd ed. Boston: Cengage Learning.

———. 2009. *The Essential Don Murray: Lessons from America's Greatest Writing Teacher,* ed. Thomas Newkirk and Lisa C. Miller. Portsmouth, NH: Heinemann.

Newkirk, Thomas. 2009. *Holding On to Good Ideas in a Time of Bad Ones: Six Literacy Principles Worth Fighting For.* Portsmouth, NH: Heinemann.

Newkirk, Thomas, and Penny Kittle. 2013. *Children Want to Write: Donald Graves and the Revolution in Children's Writing.* Portsmouth, NH: Heinemann.

Ohi, Debbie Ridpath. 2015. *Inkygirl.com.* http://inkygirl.com/dailywords.

———. 2015. Personal communication. November 8.

Overmeyer, Mark. 2015. *Let's Talk: Managing One-on-One, Peer, and Small-Group Conferences.* Portland, ME: Stenhouse.

Owocki, Gretchen, and Yetta Goodman. 2002. *Kidwatching: Documenting Children's Literacy Development.* Portsmouth, NH: Heinemann.

Price, Dan. 1999. *How to Make a Journal of Your Life.* Berkeley, CA: Ten Speed Press.

Ray, Katie Wood. 1999. *Wondrous Words: Writers and Writing in the Elementary Classroom.* Urbana, IL: National Council of Teachers of English.

———. 2002. *What You Know by Heart: How to Develop Curriculum for Your Writing Workshop*. Portsmouth, NH: Heinemann.

———. 2010. *In Pictures and In Words: Teaching the Qualities of Good Writing Through Illustration Study*. Portsmouth, NH: Heinemann.

Ray, Katie Wood, and Lester Laminack. 2001. *The Writing Workshop: Working Through the Hard Parts (and They're All Hard Parts)*. Urbana, IL: National Council of Teachers of English.

Ray, Katie Wood, and Matt Glover. 2011. *Watch Katie and Matt . . . Sit Down and Teach Up*. Portsmouth, NH: Heinemann.

Rief, Linda. 2014. *Read Write Teach: Choice and Challenge in the Reading-Writing Workshop*. Portsmouth, NH: Heinemann.

Roberts, Kate, and Maggie Beattie Roberts. 2016. *DIY Literacy: Teaching Tools for Differentiation, Rigor, and Independence*. Portsmouth, NH: Heinemann.

Rose, Sarah E., Richard P. Jolley, and Esther Burkitt. 2006. "A Review of Children's, Teachers' and Parents' Influences on Children's Drawing Experience." *International Journal of Art & Design Education* 25 (3): 341–349.

Rosenblatt, Louise. 1956. "The Acid Test for Literature Teaching." *English Journal* 11(2): 66–74.

Rosenthal, Amy Krouse. 2005. *Encyclopedia of an Ordinary Life*. New York: Three Rivers Press.

Ross, John A. 2006. "The Reliability, Validity, and Utility of Self-Assessment." *Practical Assessment, Research, & Evaluation*. 11 (10): 1–13. Available at http://pareonline.net/pdf/v11n10.pdf.

Rowell, Rainbow. N.d. "Pep Talk from Rainbow Rowell." *National Novel Writing Month*. http://nanowrimo.org/pep-talks/rainbow-rowell.

Schilling, David Russell. 2013. "Knowledge Doubling Every 12 Months, Soon to Be Every 12 Hours." *Industry Tap*. http://www.industrytap.com/knowledge-doubling-every-12-months-soon-to-be-every-12-hours/3950.

Sharp, Colby. 2013. "5,4,3,2,1 Interview Jennifer L. Holm." *Nerdy Book Club*. https://nerdybookclub.wordpress.com/2013/12/02/54321-interview-jennifer-l-holm/.

Smith, Keri. 2003. *Living Out Loud: Activities to Fuel a Creative Life*. San Francisco: Chronicle.

Spinelli, Jerry. 1998. *Knots in My Yo-Yo String*. New York: Knopf.

Tan, Shaun. 2010. "Words and Pictures, an Intimate Distance." http://www.shauntan.net/images/essayLingua-Franca.pdf.

———. 2013. *The Bird King: An Artist's Notebook*. New York: Arthur A. Levine.

Two Writing Teachers (blog). https://twowritingteachers.org.

Wilson, Maja. 2006. *Rethinking Rubrics in Writing Assessment*. Portsmouth, NH: Heinemann.

Winner, Matthew. 2016. Episode 231. *Let's Get Busy* (podcast). http://lgbpodcast.blogspot.com/.

Index

Page numbers followed by *f* indicate figures and *t* indicate tables.